Careers in
Music

Sara Peacock

**RHINEGOLD
EDUCATION**

www.rhinegoldeducation.co.uk

First published 2012 in Great Britain by
Rhinegold Education
14–15 Berners Street
London W1T 3LJ

www.musicroom.com

CAREERS IN MUSIC
Order No. RHG402
ISBN: 978-1-78038-245-6

Exclusive Distributors:
Music Sales Ltd
Distribution Centre, Newmarket Road
Bury St Edmunds, Suffolk IP33 3YB, UK

Printed in the EU

Contents

9. RETAILING 87

10. PATHWAYS AND APPLICATIONS 93

Acknowledgements
This book wouldn't have been possible without the kindness of so many people who shared their expertise and experiences – I would like to say an enormous 'thank you' to everyone who answered my questions, and to those who agreed to be featured as a case study. Special thanks must go to Mel Thornton at the Brighton Institute of Modern Music (BIMM), who provided so much information and so many contacts; to the anonymous reviewer for his or her helpful input; to Gary Downing at Music Sales for sharing his enormously wide-ranging knowledge; and to Emma Cooper and Lizzie Moore at Rhinegold Education, for all their hard work nursing the book into existence. I would also like to thank my family – my partner Angharad, and sons Jasper and Oscar – for all their support and encouragement.

Sara Peacock

Website
Throughout the book you will find www icons. Since there is so much information online, and websites change more frequently than printed information will, we have collected all sorts of useful links online for you, rather than listing them in this book. Visit www.rhinegoldeducation.co.uk/ myrhinegold and sign up; you can then register the code O9JOX3 to access further information to support the advice given here, along with links to websites that will help you in your careers research.

Foreword

I clearly remember my first experience of working in the music industry. Fresh out of university, I carried out a work placement with London Records, carrying boxes of vinyl records and bags of demos, filing, answering phones and learning how record companies work. The work was much the same as in any office but there's no denying that it was exciting seeing all the activity around their artists. At the end of my first day, I was offered VIP tickets to see my favourite band, Faith No More. I was sold on a career in music! I worked hard, developed a career as a music PR and only left five years later when headhunted by BMG to work on their pop roster of acts signed by an A&R person called Simon Cowell. I've heard he's done very well for himself.

Now I use my experience in the music industry to help music students forge a career for themselves, either as performers, songwriters, budding entrepreneurs or industry executives. I've been working as the Head of Work-based Learning at the Brighton Institute of Modern Music (BIMM) for seven years now. BIMM is the UK's leading provider of music education and I work as part of a large team of staff who are dedicated to providing students with a springboard to employment.

I've learnt a great deal from working with some truly inspirational students, as well as some of the most successful employers in the industry, and enjoyed seeing so many of our alumni succeed in their chosen field. The opportunities are endless if we keep our eyes open. The music industry is not about some large flashy offices in West London, it is all around you: we listen to music on the radio, we have easy access to gigs and festivals, and social media has enabled us to easily build communities of supporters around an artist, club night or gig.

The music industry is one of the UK's biggest and most culturally significant creative industries in the UK, employing 130,000 people. There is a range of careers for those who are committed and dedicated enough to work in this fast-paced, ever-evolving business. Behind every successful artist there is a large team of people working behind the scenes – A&R (artists and repertoire), promoters, agents, pluggers, press officers, lawyers, publishers, managers and producers, to name just a few – and this book will help you understand the key skills required for many of these roles and the best route to reaching your chosen career.

The key lessons to learn are quite simple: the music industry is a people business and soft skills are very highly valued. Those who can network, communicate and work well as part of a team will go far. Secondly, work experience is essential, whether it is a placement within a company or simply getting gigs under your belt if you're a performer. Be a self-starter; put simply, 'get involved!'

Lastly, and most importantly, remember never to lose sight of your passion for music, keep up to date with changing trends and rising stars and, most importantly of all, be yourself and enjoy your work. A job in the music industry is never just a job, it becomes part of your life. I wish all readers of this book good luck!

Mel Thornton,
Head of Work-based Learning
at BIMM Brighton.
www.bimm.co.uk

Introduction

Making and listening to music are things that most of us do for pleasure, both while growing up and as adults. But for some people it can become a career. If you are thinking that you would like to be one of those people, then this book could help you begin to choose the right path for you. Mention a career in music and many people think immediately of performing or teaching music. While these are very important avenues for musicians, there are all sorts of other creative, rewarding and challenging career paths in the music business, which is large and complex.

The UK is rightly proud of its music industry – our creative talent and the people that support them are world class. But this area – particularly recording and music retail – has undergone an enormous change since the beginning of the 21st century, with the boom in digital production, MP3 downloads and online file sharing. This book won't be able to tell you what the industry will be like in ten years' time, but aims to help you equip yourself with the skills you will need to be able to adapt to the changes that will come in the future.

The music industry can be a fun, exciting, stimulating and satisfying place to work. Because of that, it is a very popular choice for young people and the market for jobs is intensely competitive. To get your foot in the door, you will need to be determined, hard-working and very self-motivated. As well as obtaining the qualifications you need, it will be vitally important to have experience to prove to a potential employer that you are committed to the work – this could be part-time voluntary experience gained over a period of time, or a more structured work placement or internship. Depending on the career path you hope to follow, networking and self-promotion might also be important tools in your getting started in the industry (to say nothing of developing your career once you've had your first break). You will find more advice about this throughout the industry-specific chapters, as well as in the 'Pathways and Applications' chapter at the back of the book.

Increasingly, people working within the music industry are finding that they don't just have one job – more and more people are now developing a 'portfolio career', where they do a number of different roles at the same time. This could be a performer who also teaches, and works as a music examiner as well. Or perhaps a sound engineer who also DJs and teaches production in a higher education college. Sometimes this will be because one of these jobs on its own won't generate enough income to live off, but often people choose to work this way because they enjoy the variety. So, while you are thinking about which job you want to pursue, try to keep your options open and appreciate that you might be able to incorporate two, three or even more roles into your life.

In the pages that follow you will find descriptions of all sorts of jobs connected with music, hopefully including some you hadn't thought of before. There is information about what the job involves, both good and bad, what sort of qualifications you would need, what type of personality it would suit and what you need to be doing to get you started on the right path. There are also case studies from people who are already doing some of these jobs, sharing their experiences and giving advice. The last chapter gives some more general advice about qualifications and tips about looking for work.

We hope you will find all this information useful, and that it helps you to get started on your own career path. The most important thing to remember, however, is that all of the qualifications, work experience and everything else we discuss are worth nothing without the thing that you started with – your passion and love for music. Make that your primary motivation and use the advice in this book to forge your way in the music industry.

Good luck!

1. Performing

Performers are perhaps the most visible part of the music business. From concert soloists and symphony orchestra players to session musicians and pop singers, there are opportunities for people to perform in just about any style or genre. But competition is extremely fierce, and to make a career you need to have a range of skills and attributes as well as the ability to perform at the highest level. It is not an easy route to take.

If you want to make a career as a soloist, you need to be outstanding at what you do. For a lot of genres this will mean that your technical ability must be second to none; you will already have been practising hours a day, every day, for years. As well as this, though, you will need to be expressing something unique through your music – you need to have something that makes people want to listen to your interpretation rather than someone else's. Your image or the way you look might also be very important – especially for popular styles, but increasingly so in the classical music world as well.

If you want to play or sing in a group (such as in a band, or a classical ensemble or orchestra) technical ability is still important, but there are also other considerations. Classical musicians will need to be able to sight-read very well; rehearsal time is often very short and a musician or singer who can't pick the music up straight away is unlikely to be hired again. Band members will need to be collaborative, to bring something to the group rather than just follow instructions. Session musicians will need to be flexible and be able to adapt their playing to fit all sorts of different styles.

It is vitally important for any performer to be professional and reliable. This means that if you are hired for an engagement you are there on time, every time, without fail, and you must be able to perform to the same standard every single time, even in rehearsal. No one wants to pay money to hear someone who is a bit under par; there are no 'off-days' for the professional performer. You must also be able to get on with all the other people you are working with. All performances are team efforts, and if you are friendly and considerate to your fellow musicians (and all the people working behind the scenes) then you are more likely to be considered next time the organisers need to hire someone. There is also a lot of waiting around involved in any performance (waiting for lighting or soundchecks to be sorted out; waiting for other people to get their bits out of the way). You need to be patient and not the sort of person who would be stressed in this situation.

For the vast majority of working performers, travelling and antisocial hours are a big part of the job. It is highly unlikely that you will find enough work to sustain you in your home town, even if you live in a big city. You will also find yourself working a lot of nights, usually at the weekend when everyone else is out enjoying themselves. You need to be happy to relegate your social and family lives to other times and to spend a lot of time away from home in airports, train stations and hotel rooms. But most people who perform do so despite these downsides, because making a living out of the thing they love most in the world – making music and bringing pleasure to so many people – makes it all worthwhile.

SESSION MUSICIAN

About the job
Session musicians are hired on a project-by-project basis to perform music in all sorts of styles for recordings and/or performances. For recordings, you might be hired for a single particular track: perhaps a guitar band wants to use a brass section on one track of their album, or an advertising composer might want a particular combination of instruments and/or singers for a jingle. Or you might find that players are needed for tours or one-off performances.

Session musicians are required for music in every conceivable genre, so the more versatile you are the more employable you will be. If you are a guitarist, you might be asked to play blues, rock, punk, pop or country and western, for example. A singer could be asked for a classical choral sound on one track and a gospel-style backing on another. The crucial skill is to be able to deliver exactly the sound and style that the client asks for.

Qualifications and skills
Experience will be far more important than qualifications in this job, although someone looking for a classical singer or instrumentalist might like to see a traditional qualification (such as a music college performance diploma). Of utmost importance is the ability to pick up music very quickly.

ARTHUR DICK

JOB TITLE
Session musician

JOB DESCRIPTION
I play guitar – electric and acoustic. The styles vary; my preferred style is blues/jazz, but it's inspiring and fun exploring all styles.

IS THIS JOB FULL-TIME?
No: as well as playing I do a fair amount of teaching.

WHAT WAS YOUR ROUTE TO THIS JOB?
I originally began working in the Liverpool music scene, playing in various bands, touring Europe, and so on. At the same time I continued to study classical guitar and learned to read music. I took a show job, which got me into the freelance gig scene in the north west and eventually into London, where I continued with gigs and sessions as they came along. Being able to sight-read music was one of the main criteria for getting many jobs.

BEST BIT?
Playing live guitar with other musicians in a studio or a gig.

WORST BIT?
Isolation: not seeing other musicians and working enough. Times have changed in that there aren't the gigs like there used to be. Many people record at home now so the studio scene is less active. I can record at home on someone's track and then send them the file – no need to play together! It's not how music should be made.

WHAT PERSONAL QUALITIES DO YOU THINK YOU HAVE THAT HELP IN YOUR JOB?
I hope it's because people like my playing. Being sociable and flexible are important too.

WHAT PRACTICAL ADVICE WOULD YOU GIVE TO SOMEONE WHO WANTED YOUR JOB?
Try and get as much experience as you can – playing and writing with friends as well as doing the gigs you wish you didn't have to.

You might be required to sight-read, or follow tab or a lead sheet, or just pick up your part by ear – and to be perfect first time.

Another vital skill is to know the capabilities and limits of your instrument (which means your voice, for singers). Often, a composer or producer will describe the kind of sound or timbre they want and it will be up to you to produce it.

How do I start?
This is definitely a job you will learn by doing. Session drummer Michael Bowes advises: 'Get out there and get as much experience as you can' – this means playing or singing in all sorts of different circumstances, and studio experience will be vital. If you're already in a band, clubbing together for some studio time to get professional recordings of a few tracks will be good for your band as well as useful experience. Get to know the bands and groups in your area, and be the first to volunteer when they need someone, whether for live gigs or recordings. As you get to know the local studios and producers, show them how reliable and helpful you are (on top of your great playing, of course), and let them know that you're interested in session work.

RECORDING ARTIST

About the job
Perhaps you want to play or sing in a rock/pop genre, either on your own or with a band, but you want to perform your own music under your own name (not as a session musician). Being a singer (or rapper) or in a band and making it big is a dream for a lot of people, but a tiny percentage of those actually make it into a career. If you're sure you've got something special, and you're prepared to put in the hard work, then it's possible that you could be one of that tiny percentage.

The price for living your dream will be a lot of hard work, long hours and time spent away from home. You will have to be persistent and determined to get noticed, then just as persistent and determined to move on in your career. You will need to be a reliable performer – someone who's paid £30 to see a gig at the end of your long tour wants their money's worth just as much as the person who paid £30 at the beginning of the tour when you were fresh. A performer with a good technique will be able to keep producing sparkling performances, no matter how tired they are; a performer who burns out and lets people down won't last very long in the business.

There are other aspects to consider as well, depending on the genre of music and how 'big' you want to become. You may find that if you sign a deal with a recording company they might want to change your image to make you appeal more to what they think is your target market. You might also find yourself in the public eye, so this could mean a loss of privacy as well as journalists feeling they can comment on you or the way you look – this is a part of being famous, so you will have to be comfortable with this possibility.

Qualifications

Really the only qualification here is to be able to do it – to perform (and perhaps write) music that people want to listen to. So to begin with you need to be talented, but that really is just the first step. You will need to develop your technique, so that means practice – a lot of it! Depending on your instrument and style, you might find the grade exams such as those run by Rockschool or Trinity College London a good framework for helping you to improve your technique. For some types of music, the ability to dance will also come in useful – probably more so for R&B than country and western! In this case, you might find that a performing arts course will help you develop the skills you need, or it might just be that you spend all your spare time practising to develop your technique.

How do I get started?

Make sure that you are listening, critically, to a lot of other artists and using that to reflect on what you can improve with your own performances. Think about the recording industry as well – where would your music fit in? Practise for at least a couple of hours every single day, listening carefully to yourself and concentrating particularly on bits that you think could be improved. Try to get the chance to perform for other people whose judgement you trust and use their feedback to help you improve further. Take any opportunity to perform your music – showcase nights, gigs at the local pub, student events, or perhaps even put on your own gigs. Work on building up your local fan base – if you're looking for a recording contract, a company will want to see that you have good local support before they start.

When you have a body of music – perhaps ten or more songs – get a demo recording made. Some bands book time in a professional studio, which can be a very educational experience. Others find that the improving quality of domestic recording equipment means that they can make their own demos (although only go down this route if you have the technical know-how and equipment to do a good job of it; an amateurish demo will be no help to you at all). When you have a demo, you can start to send it to agents, record company A&Rs, and so on. In addition, get your recordings up on a public site such as SoundCloud or Facebook and all the other music/social networking sites you can. Encourage your local fans to share your music with their friends.

Few recording companies now will accept unsolicited demo recordings, so you will need to find other ways to get the A&R executives to notice you. Building up a good local following for live performances is a good first step – you could send your demos to local journalists and music reviewers and try to get positive attention in the press. Getting some airplay on the radio is another goal – you could target local radio stations, and also try to get involved with BBC Introducing (www.bbc.co.uk/introducing).

A website is also going to be essential. You will be able to upload information about yourselves and pictures, along with a few demo recordings. It's then just a short step to using this to sell your music direct to the public. This is a route a number of artists follow before getting a recording contract, and some then develop this into their own independent label, choosing not to go with the bigger labels at all. If you choose to go down this route, there will be an awful lot more to learn about music production, marketing, distribution and so on (distribution will be particularly key).

Tim Elsenburg from the band Sweet Billy Pilgrim has this advice for aspiring performers:

> In practical terms, I'd say get as many fingers into as many pies as you can! Don't be snobby or too single-minded; it's all music and it's all a chance to grow and learn that will feed into whatever you do. TV music, library music, co-writing, remixing, producing, playing with other musicians ... just jump in and don't worry about the money. Keep your personal projects as your focus, of course, but be curious ... ask questions ... write to people and then spend as much time as humanly possible getting good at what you do. I read somewhere that all of those people who have had an impact on the world via their talent have invested upwards of 10,000 hours of time in getting good at it (that translates to about 10 years). There are no real shortcuts.

> Above all though, don't do it for the money! Do it because without it in your life you're not truly you.

DJ

This section is about club DJs; for radio DJs see the Broadcasting chapter.

About the job
Back in the twentieth century, a DJ was someone who played the records at a disco and perhaps talked in between. Out of this grew the art of turntablism, and the role of the DJ moved on to a new artistic level. As a club DJ, you will still be playing records for people to dance to, but you will probably now also be creative with those sounds, incorporating effects and mixing to create your own pieces of music.

A club DJ is still responsible for keeping people on the dance floor, of course – you have to be very good at judging the reactions of your crowd to give them music to keep them dancing, knowing exactly what to play and when. You also have to be technically minded and able to deal with all the equipment (the decks, mixer, microphone, etc.). In addition, some DJs with advanced turntablism skills provide the beats for MCs and rappers, both live and in recordings. A lot of DJs working in the recording industry now use digital recordings and computer software to create the sounds using samples, loops, and so on.

Qualifications
To begin with, you will need to develop the skills to work the necessary technical equipment. There are courses in turntablism for starters (and you can offer it as a performance option for A-level music); you will need to invest in your own equipment and practise like mad. You will also need to start your own collection of recordings, whether you choose to go down the vinyl or digital route.

You might also find it very useful to learn or teach yourself to use a digital audio workstation, running software such as Cubase.

How do I get started?
Once you've acquired your equipment and your recordings, you will need to practise, and then practise some more. You will need to do your research, which means checking out the clubs in your area, the music they play, the people that go there. Take every opportunity to watch other DJs and learn from them. Once you've developed your technique, you can practise by DJing parties for friends, or perhaps for student events.

MAX RAYMOND

JOB TITLE
DJ

JOB DESCRIPTION
I play music in bars and clubs in London. My job as a DJ is to entertain an audience. This may range from just playing background music in a trendy retail shop, to keeping a dance floor busy in a late night East London club. It all depends on the venue and how the audience reacts to the music during the set. Most promoters will tell the DJ prior to the set. I mainly play an eclectic set in bars (nu disco, old hip hop, pop etc) and more of a higher tempo set in clubs (house, dance etc).

WHAT WAS YOUR ROUTE TO THIS JOB?
I started as a 'bedroom DJ' aged 14, and once I had mastered the basics I moved on to playing a friend's party. Going from being a 'bedroom DJ' to getting paid work can be difficult. I started off by going along to a friend's gig and helping out with the odd mix. After a few months of this, the promoter asked if I could fill in when one of his DJs was ill. From there I became a resident DJ, and once you have a residency it's much easier to get other paid work.

BEST BIT?
Seeing people enjoying themselves.

WORST BIT?
The worst part of my job is when people, who are a little worse for wear, ask for stupid requests. For example, when a person comes over and requests three songs by the same artist and demands for them to be played one after the other. This only really happens during bar gigs.

WHAT PERSONAL QUALITIES DO YOU THINK YOU HAVE THAT HELP IN YOUR JOB?
Good rhythm and an eclectic taste in music.

Get yourself known at the clubs that play the sort of music you like and get to know the other DJs there and the promoters. Put together demo mixes to show the music you like (and how well you can mix), and use these to show them what you can do. If you get offered a trial slot at the club, it will probably be an early one (when the club is usually quite quiet); persuade as many of your friends as possible to come along to support you, to show the club management you can bring people in.

CHORAL SINGER

About the job
There are a small number of professional choirs, but places in them are limited and highly competitive. You will need to have a very strong background in choral singing, and be able to sight-read even the most complex and difficult music flawlessly. For men, there are also opportunities for lay clerks (singers) with some cathedral and church choirs. None of these jobs is likely to be a full-time commitment, so would need to be juggled with other occupations in order to provide a full income.

Qualifications and skills
A music qualification would be an advantage here – whether from a university or a music college. Many choristers have qualifications in entirely unrelated areas but have developed their musical skills in extracurricular study so have practical qualifications (e.g. Grade 8, diploma) in music. As well as the sight-reading mentioned above, a choir's conductor wants to see someone who has an excellent ear and can blend with the other voices around them, who knows how to adapt their style and timbre to fit

different periods and genres of music, and who follows instructions and delivers what the conductor asks for. Most importantly, a chorister has to be a team player – divas are definitely not welcomed.

How do I start?
It's never too early to start choral singing; many church choirs take children from as young as eight years old, and choristers at cathedrals get a very early taste of what it is like to perform professionally. There are many choral opportunities for students in university/college choirs and (for men) in cathedral choirs – a number of British universities offer choral scholarships to students in return for regular singing in chapel services. Further experience can be obtained by working as a 'dep', filling in places in church and cathedral choirs while the permanent members are away. It is then a question of keeping an eye out for auditions for a permanent place in a choir. See the Rhinegold Education website for ideas of where to look for audition notices.

OPERA SINGER

About the job
Opera companies use singers for both the solo roles and chorus work. A chorus job can be permanent, with one organisation; the solo roles are more likely to be on a fixed-term basis for a single production or season. As well as an excellent voice and stamina, you will need to be good at acting and stagecraft – perhaps even have dancing skills. You will be expected to turn up to rehearsals note- and word-perfect, to be able to tackle anything from Bach to Bellini to Boulez, and to be comfortable singing in English, Italian, German, French, Russian and Czech, at the least.

Opera is very much an international field, so you may have to be prepared to travel for work. Even if you are lucky enough to find a permanent chorus position close to home, you will still have to go away on tour. Soloists may find that they are away from home most of the time. The job also entails a lot of waiting around. As Claire Pascoe, chorister with Opera North, advises: 'Develop a hobby; it'll keep you going while you are travelling all over the place and waiting at the back of rehearsal rooms.'

A lot of singers who perform in opera also find work as concert soloists for oratorio work with choirs and orchestras. These are usually one-off performances to be fitted in around other work. Calm professionalism is required here – you need to know the piece you are going to perform inside out, and you may find that you only have one rehearsal in which to get to know the conductor and his or her interpretation of the work.

Qualifications and skills

Developing the technique to be able to produce an operatic-quality voice and sustain that over time without damage takes years of practice and expert tuition. Opera singers will also have to study languages, acting and movement, as well as having a good all-round knowledge of music. Operatic singers are usually advised not to try to develop an operatic voice too early, so a lot of singers go on to serious study a little later than instrumentalists – perhaps in their early twenties. A great many will go through the conservatoire system (for example, Claire Pascoe, quoted above, went on to the Royal Academy of Music for four years after gaining a degree in history at university), but others will study privately with a first-rate teacher to get to the same level. Some of the music colleges offer specialised opera courses, which cover all the other elements as well as vocal technique.

How do I start?

While you are developing your voice, take every opportunity to perform both in oratorio and staged work; to begin with, this will be on a voluntary basis, but you can offer your services to local amateur choirs and choral societies. This is all excellent experience. Whether you study at a conservatoire or privately, there will come a point when your teacher advises that you are ready to audition for professional work, and should be able to point you in the right direction.

Claire Pascoe gives the following advice for those starting out:

By the time you get to this level everyone is good. This means that there's a certain amount of luck at being the right voice at the right time, but you can maximise this by going for every audition you can. A caveat is: don't audition if you're unwell – if you sing badly and it could have been avoided you'll kick yourself. It doesn't matter how many times you tell people you have a cold, if someone else is healthy and they sing better than you, they'll get the job and the panel will only remember how you sang, not why.

Music competitions are another good way to gain experience and raise your profile. Perhaps the best-known one for singers is the BBC Cardiff

MICHAEL BENNETT

JOB TITLE
Freelance opera singer.

JOB DESCRIPTION
I work as an opera and concert singer in the UK and across Europe, particularly France and Germany.

WHAT WAS YOUR ROUTE TO THIS JOB?
I started singing at the age of six in my local choir and two years later I became a chorister at Westminster Abbey. I continued to sing in school choirs after leaving Westminster and then was awarded a choral scholarship at university, where I also studied singing privately. My teacher suggested I audition for a place at music college; I received an entrance scholarship to study at the Royal Northern College of Music and spent six years there training to become a singer. After leaving I successfully auditioned for small companies in the UK such as Pimlico Opera, as well as understudying several roles for English National Opera. In 1998 I auditioned for the festival in Aix-en-Provence and was accepted on their young artist programme, which opened up many doors for me in Europe.

BEST BIT?
Being paid to do something that I love doing! Travelling, working in some beautiful places, meeting new and often inspiring people, discovering new music, working with living composers (I perform a lot of modern music) and not having a fixed routine week after week.

WORST BIT?
Travelling (it can also be exhausting), working with difficult people, spending weeks on end in a hotel, stress, nerves, stage fright (not the same as nerves), memorising music, being away from home and from friends and family, sustaining a relationship with my family by phone or internet (though Skype has improved my work lifestyle in recent years). Insecurity about work and money, auditioning, critics!

WHAT PERSONAL QUALITIES DO YOU THINK YOU HAVE THAT HELP IN YOUR JOB?
Independence: in this job you can often find yourself feeling lonely, a long way from home for weeks at a time, and you need to be resilient and not be bored of

your own company. I think I'm quite an open-minded and outgoing person, and that probably helps in this job as you find yourself thrown together with complete strangers away from home and you have to work very closely and intensely with them, which is not always easy.

WHAT PRACTICAL ADVICE WOULD YOU GIVE TO SOMEONE WHO WANTED YOUR JOB?

Learn to be self-disciplined! There are limits to how many hours a day you can actually sing, but there are no limits to how much work you can do connected to singing such as learning languages, memorising music, studying text, etc.

Singer of the World competition, held every two years. Not everyone is happy about the competitive aspect of them, but there is the chance to have valuable feedback from well-established professionals and perhaps even financial reward.

Consider looking abroad for both training and work opportunities: in comparison to the rest of Europe, there are relatively few work opportunities in the UK and they are not as well paid!

CLASSICAL INSTRUMENTALIST

About the job

If you want to have a career performing on an orchestral instrument, there are all sorts of opportunities with orchestras throughout the UK and Europe (and even further afield). There are also chamber groups of various sizes, or you might choose to set up a group of your own. Being an orchestral player is not glamorous – there is a lot of waiting around involved, as well as frequent touring, and the pay is not wonderful – but it's regular work and many people enjoy the camaraderie of working with a large group. Players in chamber ensembles may find that they need to do a lot of their own promotion and administration.

A permanent position with an orchestra can provide a level of security relatively rare in the world of performing, and there is the opportunity also to move through the ranks and become section leader. But many orchestral players still find the need to combine their playing with teaching, or another source of additional income. Other players fit together a variety of playing with different orchestras and chamber groups along with solo work.

As well as symphony orchestras, there are orchestras needed by permanent, and touring, ballet and opera companies, as well as smaller orchestras such as the Scarborough Spa Orchestra. Some West End and touring musicals will also want orchestral musicians.

Qualifications and skills
Instrumentalists will need to have studied at a conservatoire, or at least have had private study with a top-flight teacher to the same standard. As much experience as possible of orchestral playing is vital – there are opportunities for younger players in the National Children's Orchestra, various county youth orchestras and the National Youth Orchestra. It is expected that players auditioning for places in orchestras know all the standard orchestral pieces, and they will be asked to play specific excerpts as part of their audition.

How do I start?
Getting a Grade 8 distinction is the first basic step for an instrumentalist. You will probably go on to a conservatoire, or continue study with a teacher of that standard, in addition to practising at least five hours a day while you gain a good overall knowledge of the repertoire for your instrument. During study you will also have the opportunity to find out what sort of playing suits you best and whether you are going to pursue a career as a soloist, chamber player or orchestral player (or perhaps in a niche such as performance on period instruments). A number of chamber groups are in fact formed while the players are at a conservatoire together.

If orchestral playing is your choice, when the time comes you will need to start auditioning. Individual orchestras will advertise places on their own websites, and there are also sites that post notices of advertisements from orchestras all over the world.

There are various grants and opportunities for young instrumentalists and singers to help them get their careers started, such as the Countess of Munster Trust and the BBC Radio 3 Young Artists Scheme.

CONDUCTOR

There are opportunities for conductors at all sorts of levels, from being paid to rehearse and conduct a local choral society, to being the guest conductor of a large symphony orchestra. As well as an excellent musical education,

RUMON GAMBA

JOB TITLE
Conductor

JOB DESCRIPTION
Leading rehearsals and performances with orchestras and opera companies worldwide.

WHAT WAS YOUR ROUTE TO THIS JOB?
I studied cello and piano, and took a music degree. While I was finishing postgraduate conducting studies (and conducting student, amateur and youth orchestras), I won the first BBC Young Musicians Young Conductors Workshop; that led to a lot of work, which thankfully hasn't stopped since!

BEST BIT?
Being able to do something I really love (and always dreamed of) as my day job. Making music almost every day with a very large group of people and being able to share that with a (hopefully) happy and satisfied audience.

WORST BIT?
Being away from my home and family.

WHAT PERSONAL QUALITIES DO YOU THINK YOU HAVE THAT HELP IN YOUR JOB?
Being strong-minded/-willed – one must have a clear idea of what one wants and a determination to get it. Mix that with a little Latin red-blood to allow heart to assist head and inspire performances of spontaneity and creative energy. A positive and genial nature, for me, is essential to bring the best out of a group of people.

WHAT PRACTICAL ADVICE WOULD YOU GIVE TO SOMEONE WHO WANTED YOUR JOB?
Go and watch orchestras and conductors in action, especially in rehearsal. Have an idea/feeling about how every bar, every note in a piece should be.

conductors need to have a deep understanding of musical structure, and the passion and ability to transmit that to singers and instrumentalists at the appropriate level with just the right level of authority and tact. There is also a technique to acquire, and young conductors spend a long time learning the 'nuts and bolts' that transmit their ideas to the musicians as they develop their own style of putting that across.

Qualifications and skills

Some conductors come from a performance background or from instrumental/singing studies at a conservatoire; others from an academic one, studying music at university. Whichever educational route is chosen, you will need to have instilled a very deep understanding of the way music works, along with the practical skill of being able to read a (sometimes very large) score and 'hear' it. A conductor is 'playing' the orchestra or choir – they need to have the right vocabulary, as well as the communication and physical skills to be able to share with the musicians the interpretation they feel for the piece of music. Conservatoires offer postgraduate courses in conducting.

How do I start?

The most important place to begin is getting to know music inside-out; the study of musical history, performance practice and harmony, for example. While studying, experience of conducting can be gained with student choirs and orchestras, and local amateur groups. Keep an eye on orchestras' websites for assistant conductor positions.

PIANIST/RÉPÉTITEUR

About the job

As well as working as solo performers, classical pianists can find work in chamber groups and also as accompanists. Each of these roles needs a slightly different approach; some will like the autonomy of being solely responsible for the musical interpretation, while others will prefer the collaborative aspect of working as an accompanist or in a chamber ensemble.

The job of répétiteur is a particularly niche occupation for a highly skilled pianist. Ballet, opera and musical theatre companies, as well as some choirs, use a pianist to play for the majority of rehearsals, not bringing the orchestra in until the last moment; ballet companies will also want a pianist for their daily classes. Often, though, the répétiteur will not be playing music that has been adapted for the piano – they will be expected to read from the full orchestral score, so have to do their own adaptation as they go along (representing the harmony, rhythm, important melodies, and so on) – obviously, this means transposing a number of lines as well. The répétiteur needs to follow the conductor exactly, to be supportive to the main performers, to jump to exactly the spot the conductor (or choreographer) wants to go from, and so on.

ORGANIST

Organists are employed by all of the major cathedrals in the UK, along with some of the larger churches. Their role is to accompany the choir and congregation at services, as well as at other events such as weddings and funerals. Often the organist is also expected to train and conduct the choir. The job requires a daily commitment to attend services, but is not enough on its own to provide a full-time income so needs to be combined with other forms of employment, such as teaching. There are a few opportunities also for organists to perform solo recitals or to fill in the occasional organ part in orchestral works, but these are quite rare.

The Royal College of Organists provides structured examinations for aspiring organists, and smaller parish churches will often employ young people to play for services while they are learning the organ. A number of universities and churches around the UK have organ scholarships available to students, who then play regularly for services as they are studying.

OTHER OPPORTUNITIES TO PERFORM

About the job
The most common performance roles have been covered here, but there are also other opportunities for performers, either individually or in groups.

One important source of employment is as a function band or a tribute band, providing entertainment for weddings, parties, corporate events, and so on. The key to being a successful function band is to get a good live agent, most of whom have a broad roster of artists on their books. These agents are always looking to fill their roster's requirements so that they can always offer a service when people call looking for entertainment. Getting an agent isn't easy and function bands work in a strictly commercial environment. To find the standard that agents are looking for, visit the websites for function band agencies such as Psycho and Alive Network.

Many cafes, bars and restaurants enjoy having live music as an attraction for their customers – whether it's a jazz quartet for a restaurant, a pianist playing standards for a wine bar, a rock band playing at the regular gig night in a pub, or a string quartet playing for afternoon tea at an upmarket hotel. It is unlikely that these will be advertised – it will be up to you to advertise your services and seek out opportunities, perhaps by taking round a demo recording of what you can do. Some of these places will expect you to play for free – it will be up to you to decide whether it will be worth your while to do this for the exposure it can give you.

Cruise ships often have openings for entertainers of many varieties, which can be excellent training in the regular production of consistent performances. Perhaps not a good option for those who don't have their sea legs! Similarly, hotels and large resorts – both in the UK and abroad – sometimes have opportunities for musical entertainers. Musicians are also sometimes employed at large corporate events and at weddings.

None of these alone could provide a long-term career for a performer, but they could be income-generating activities for those beginning to get their careers off the ground, or sidelines to run alongside other occupations.

2. Composing

As long as we have had music, people have always made a living by creating it for other people's enjoyment. Hildegard von Bingen wrote music for her nuns to sing in church in the Middle Ages; Joseph Haydn wrote music for the entertainment of his patrons in the eighteenth century; two hundred years later, Burt Bacharach wrote songs for some of the most popular performers of his day to sing. Today, we are lucky enough to enjoy a huge range of different types of music, and people compose music to be used in all sorts of situations.

Today, a composer could be someone who writes operas, pop songs, or the music for advertisements, films, TV programmes or even video games. All of these types of music have their own demands and limitations, but all need composers who are imaginative and hard-working.

For very few people does a piece of music appear fully formed in the mind – most will have the germ of an idea and then spend a long time developing and perfecting the piece of music that grows out of it. As composer, songwriter and producer Joel Cadbury says, 'A good idea generally forms quickly but the devil is in the detail, and that's what can take the time.' Most young musicians these days have had experience of composing, as well as performing, because it is now a compulsory part of the GCSE and A-level music examinations. If you have enjoyed your composing experience, and feel that you could consistently come up with ideas as well as have the dedication to develop them, a career in composition could be enormously rewarding.

There are composition skills to be learned and developed, but turning these into gainful employment might depend on your networking skills. Joel Cadbury again says:

> It seems to me that this is all about meeting the right people at the right time. I don't think I have ever got a job though a website or magazine; every time it seems to be about a face-to-face meeting with someone at a time when they need what I can provide. Knowing people in the right fields is crucial. There is always someone out there that needs what you

can deliver; it's all about developing those connections. Luck does play a part in this but with the right commitment a path can be carved out.

CLASSICAL COMPOSITION

About the job
There are a small number of 'classical' composers in the UK, who create music for choirs, orchestras, chamber groups and soloists to perform in concerts and recordings. Some of these composers are at the cutting edge of technological innovation, working with computers and other electronic devices to push at the boundaries of what music does and how it is created.

This branch of composition is part of a tradition going back hundreds of years, and so most of its composers will come from an academic background (having studied with other composers at a university or conservatoire). Many will continue to work from within one of these institutions, passing on their skills and legacy by teaching other composition students. Many classical composers find that the income can be very erratic, and the difficulty in obtaining commissions and opportunities to work with large-scale forces very frustrating. Also, not everyone appreciates the often solitary lifestyle of the composer.

Qualifications
Classical composers are expected to have a deep knowledge and understanding of the Western classical repertoire, including detailed knowledge of harmony, orchestration and music history. This usually means they will have at least an undergraduate degree in music. Many people then go on to study composition at a postgraduate level, often as a PhD, studying with another composer in the field. A lot of composers also have another string to their bow, perhaps as a performer or a conductor.

Those composers choosing to specialise in electroacoustic music will also need excellent technical ability and knowledge of sound production techniques and computing. Composers who manage to obtain a post-doctoral position within a university music department or conservatoire will probably find that they are expected to publish research in journals or books as well as teach, so they will need to develop skills in writing words as well as music.

PROFESSOR PAUL MEALOR

JOB TITLE
Composer and professor of composition at the University of Aberdeen.

JOB DESCRIPTION
I compose music! Often vocal and choral music, but also orchestral, chamber music and songs. I compose every morning, then go for a long walk and use that time to mull over what I've written, go back to my desk and write some more, then go to my job at Aberdeen University and try to teach others how to write.

IS THIS JOB FULL-TIME?
As I am a composer and university professor of composition, the two jobs are interlinked and feed off each other. It might seem strange, but in teaching others I can often find solutions to my own compositional problems.

WHAT WAS YOUR ROUTE TO THIS JOB?
I started composing at the age of nine, after a spiritual experience – I almost drowned in a river near our home and had an epiphany! I knew that I had to compose. I then had early lessons in composition from William Mathias and John Pickard before reading music at the University of York (BA, 1997 and PhD, 2002) and at the Royal Danish Academy of Music (1998–99). All of this training really gave me a good grounding in compositional technique.

BEST BIT?
I love waking up in the morning and knowing that I will compose! I adore thinking up melodies and working out the structure and emotional content of a piece. I love every aspect of my job.

WORST BIT?
Nothing at all! I have the dream job!

WHAT PERSONAL QUALITIES DO YOU THINK YOU HAVE THAT HELP IN YOUR JOB?
You need to have an inner drive and energy, and need to want to compose so much that you couldn't live without it. You need a creative buzz, musical ideas, and the training that can help you shape those ideas. Get lots of training from many teachers. Become like a sponge, absorbing all advice.

How do I get started?

A strong 'traditional' music education background is needed for this career path. This means A-level music, perhaps accompanied by music theory qualifications and a Grade 8 in an instrument, followed by a music degree. During all of this education, keep writing music, and take every opportunity to have it performed by your school orchestra, county youth choir, student string quartet – whoever you can find. Talk to the performers to find out what they like or don't like about the music; what is difficult or pleasurable to play. Make recordings of your music so that you can start to create a portfolio of your compositions. Listen to as much 'new' music as you can – live, on the radio and on recordings, and try to learn from what other people are writing.

FILM AND TV MUSIC

About the job

Nearly all the programmes and films we watch on screen have some kind of music in them. For some television programmes this could be the theme music at the beginning and end, but for some feature films this could be 90 minutes or so of almost continuous music. This can be a very rewarding, and sometimes pressured and stressful, career for a composer. For this sort of composition you need to have a very good idea of the emotional impact of your music and how it can work with what the director is presenting visually.

Composers for moving pictures very rarely have free rein to compose whatever they feel like. Most of the time they will have a very clear brief from the programme or film's director, which might include the emotional feel the scene is trying to create, the moments in the action that need to be punctuated or even perhaps hints at other things that will happen later in the action.

Often, the music will need to be composed to a strict time brief so as to fit the action. Some film composers develop a style of music that can be extended or cut unobtrusively, to make it easier to fit the music to the action. Often, the film editing stage will mean that a scene loses or gains a few seconds right at the end of the production process, and the composer will need to be able to adjust their music to match very quickly and with very little notice.

Film/TV editors and production companies also use stock 'library' music, which they will use either to provide temporary musical accompaniment to early edits of the action, or to be broadcast as part of the programme. These are licensed by companies such as Audio Network or EMI Production Music.

Qualifications
As long as you have the right skills and experience, there aren't any particular qualifications that are necessary for this job, and many composers come into this sort of work from being performers themselves and developing their skill in a practical context. Some might come from an academic composition background, and there are now some dedicated film-composition courses that can offer a mixture of academic learning and practical experience, specially geared towards the types of skills the film composer needs.

How do I get started?
Keep composing as much as you can, and experiment with adapting something you have written to different contexts – could it work as a 30-second theme tune? Could you make it work under a love scene, a chase sequence, a moment of tension? Could you cut it by five seconds or expand it by ten?

Do as much research as you can. A lot of film music is available on sound-track recordings, so you can do close listening without visual distractions to hear how it is structured, the orchestration that is used, and so on. But listen to it also with the visuals it was intended for so that you can learn how the two work together to produce an effect.

When you are starting out, get to know people who are also starting out in video production (writers, directors, producers, and so on) – for example, collaborating with film students on their productions is a great way to

GUY FARLEY

JOB TITLE
Film composer

JOB DESCRIPTION:
I compose, arrange, orchestrate and produce music for motion picture, including TV, commercials, concert arrangements, songs and film scores.

WHAT WAS YOUR ROUTE TO THIS JOB?
Luck and opportunity, created by being in the right place at the right time. A friend made a short thriller film and because he knew I wrote music he asked me to write for his film. The director of photography on that film made a film himself some years later and he came to me to ask me to write music. Then came his cousin and finally a director through recommendation. All I did was to make myself available, do whatever they required with enthusiasm and efficiency, write music of excellent quality, deliver on time and within budget, and solve the production of music for the film-makers.

BEST BIT?
The day I stand in front of a 70-piece orchestra, raise my baton and hear the first notes of the music that I wrote weeks or sometimes months before on a piano. Nothing beats this!

WORST BIT?
The pressure of time and production is first: on a big score (90 minutes of music, for example) the pressure to write every day and meet deadlines is uncomfortable. Then it is being told what to write by producers or directors who don't understand music or even the process of composing.

WHAT PERSONAL QUALITIES DO YOU THINK YOU HAVE THAT HELP IN YOUR JOB?
Getting on with people – adapting to them and understanding them while being able to communicate your feelings and the issues of music production; humility – knowing your place and not trying to impose your opinions on others; quietly getting the job done without fuss or creating mayhem; being a problem solver; ensuring that the producers and director have complete faith in you and your ability to make their film better, and without production issues.

practise your skills and get used to what's involved with the job. It's also a good way to make contacts with future film- and programme-makers.

As this career will mean always juggling a number of different projects, direct your energy in a number of different areas. Composer James Williams recommends:

Have three projects moving forward in the public domain (anywhere from the local pub venue to national television) at one time. The projects needn't be huge: perhaps your own band, guesting with another band, offering music for a short student film, a part-time internship somewhere, and so on. When one project goes down, replace it with something new and any positive energy that the old project has generated (a following, contacts, reputation, etc.) will be transferred onto the next project and so on. If your stuff is out there and being seen or heard, it doesn't feel that people are clocking it all the time, but you'd be surprised at the extent to which they take note if the stuff is good.

OTHER KINDS OF COMPOSING

Advertisements
This is a specialised branch of the television composer's role. Music for adverts needs to be short and catchy. Most importantly, the composer needs to be able to represent the ad agency's ideas for the product in sound, which is no mean feat. If you think this might be something you would like to try, practise writing short pieces of music, no more than

30 seconds long, that illustrate something very specific, such as 'spring meadow with wild flowers' or 'urban decay', and aim to make them as distinctive and memorable as possible; try to use a different style or genre of music for each one.

Video games
Another niche sector of moving-pictures composing is that for the rapidly growing video game sector. As well as having all the skills mentioned above that are needed for a film and TV composer, you will need to be a gamer yourself. This is a distinct genre with its own conventions, and you will have to understand these well to be able to write music for them.

Songwriter
Often people who start out a career as a singer-songwriter, or as the main composer in a band, will end up writing songs for other people to perform. Or it might just be that songwriting is where your passion is, and you don't necessarily want to perform yourself. Some songwriters create both words and music; others find a collaborator to write the words while they create the music. If you want to write songs, though, you need to get them 'out there' so you'll either need to perform them yourself, or get someone else to do it for you, and work towards getting the attention of music publishing and/or recording companies. Jon Webster, Chief Executive of the Music Managers Forum, suggests: 'Try using social networking to look for artists who don't write or who want to co-write, or if you see an artist you like playing live ... then ask if you can co-write with them.' Most songwriters, though, have a career after they have had a hit track; that first hit is the hard one to get. It is very important to make sure that your compositions are copyrighted and registered with the proper societies, such as the PRS, ASCAP, and so on.

Musical theatre
Writing music for the theatre, whether incidental music for plays or full-blown musicals, is another possible area of employment for a composer. As with film and TV music if this is an area you are interested in, it is a good idea to get to know the conventions of the theatre and learn from composers who have gone before. Although the number of composers who manage to get a full musical produced, let alone a West-End smash hit, is relatively small, it could be a good line of interest to have running alongside other composition projects.

Educational materials

Some writers of musicals have success developing their ideas for schools and young people to perform; shows that are written for the resources and talents of young people are often welcomed by schools and youth groups. Every year, compositions written specifically for children and music learners are published – perhaps as songbooks to be used in class-rooms or small pieces for beginner instrumentalists. You will need to have a good idea of what level of technique is appropriate for each of these, so some background in teaching would probably be useful alongside your composition skills.

Orchestration

Musicians who are adept in orchestration skills might also be able to find work adapting compositions that already exist for different forces, including full orchestra. The demand for this sort of work exists across all kinds of areas, including film/TV work, advertising, video games and musical theatre. As well as the necessary skills in instrumentation, orchestrators may find that they need to be adept with the relevant technology (such as digital audio workstation programmes and sampling techniques).

3. Teaching

Many people see teaching as a vocation or a 'calling', rather than just a career. There used to be a saying: 'those who can, do; those who can't, teach'. But nothing could be further from the truth: to be a teacher you need to be able to 'do', and a whole lot more besides. If you are passionate about music and think that you can pass that on to other people, whether children or adults, then teaching might be the option for you. But it isn't something just to fall into if you are a failed performer, or can't think what else to do. Teachers have the opportunity to make a difference to people's lives, and it is a vitally important career which demands a variety of skillsets and personality traits.

There is a well-established music education structure in the UK, from parent-and-baby music groups right through to music appreciation or history classes for retired people, and every age and standard in between. There are also opportunities to work with groups or one-on-one, and you might find that you prefer one or the other situation, or a mixture of both.

Whatever style of teaching you go into, there are a number of attributes you will need. Patience is vital; every student will work at their own pace and a short-tempered teacher isn't going to help most of them (although some students will respond well to firm discipline – but that isn't necessarily the same thing as being short-tempered). Flexibility and empathy are also useful: if you can see why a student isn't quite 'getting' the point you are making, or isn't able to make a particular bit of technique work for them, and you can find a different way to approach the situation, you will be able to help more people progress. Your personality will inform your teaching style; with experience you will find the model that works best for you and helps you to get the most from your students.

Teaching can be very hard work. If you are teaching in a school, you will find that you put in far more hours than most of your colleagues in other subjects as there are all sorts of extracurricular groups that you will need to run in lunchtimes and after school on top of your usual class-teaching work. Private teachers (such as one-on-one instrumental teachers) will find themselves working a lot of evenings and perhaps weekends, as most people will want to come for lessons outside of work or school hours.

The rewards for all of this hard work can be enormous. Of course you will be proud if your star pupil goes on to have a hit single or gets a place at a conservatoire, but most of the pleasure from teaching is going to be from sharing the joy of others as they incorporate music into their life and achieve their goals, whatever those may be. Making music needs to be an inclusive activity; if you can get the right balance of encouraging participation as well as excellence you could be making a huge difference to people's lives.

SCHOOL TEACHING

About the job
Music is included in the National Curriculum for all areas of the UK. Primary schools usually employ a music specialist who is a general class teacher but who takes responsibility for the provision of music in the school, and sometimes due to funding this may only be part time. A significant number of non-specialists also take music lessons at primary level. This can be daunting for someone with no music experience, and so your musical skills will be warmly welcomed should you become a primary teacher. Secondary school music teachers will focus on that subject alone (although some schools do employ teachers to 'double up' and teach more than one subject if they are suitably qualified). Teachers in both age sectors will be expected to organise and run extracurricular groups (choir, orchestra, bands, and so on) on top of their usual teaching; there will be more of this at secondary level than at primary.

In schools, teaching music is not just about helping people learn to play an instrument or sing. At primary level, you will be helping children to learn about the basic building-blocks of music: rhythm, melody, putting different elements together to create harmony and texture, and so on. At secondary level the knowledge gets increasingly specialised. For GCSEs and A levels you will need to be able to teach about the whole span of music history, as well as the rules of harmony; you will have to be able to help develop young people's skill as composers as well as support them as they perform (this could include classical piano or turntablism – any genre or discipline). Teachers need to be able to engage a range of interests among their pupils, using the music they are listening to in order to teach the skills and elements of music. So it's very important to be willing to deal with a diverse range of music, and to encourage students to do the same. As one secondary school music teacher notes, 'any music teacher educating students beyond GCSE level will need to have an excellent musical knowledge on all aspects of the subject'.

There is also increasingly a need to be adept with technology, as pupils can use computer programs to produce, manipulate and record their compositions and performances. It's not just computers either, as all sorts of other devices (tablets, mobile devices, and so on) become capable of manipulating music. If you have a background in this sort of technology, that will be really useful; if not, you will need to be prepared to put in some extra work to learn to use it.

There are also the general skills that any teacher within a mainstream school will need – the ability to control and manage groups of approximately 30 pupils at a time; the creation of interesting and engaging lesson plans that deliver the set curriculum; differentiation of the material being taught so that slower learners are supported and faster learners have extension tasks that enrich or broaden that lesson; and knowledge of how to cope with and help pupils with special educational needs. There may well be a certain amount of extra administration – for example, organising the peripatetic teachers who come in to school to teach instruments and singing, 'recruiting' pupils to take lessons, making sure they know what time to be there, and so on.

Outside of the classroom, the music teacher's role is also demanding, as extracurricular activities should promote both participation and excellence. If you are blessed with a school full of talented musicians then of course they should have the opportunity to show what they can do; you will need to provide them with the framework to make music together (in an orchestra, band, chamber group, choir – whatever fits the musicians you have). But the musicians who are just starting to learn, or who just find it harder to progress as quickly, also deserve to have their chance to make music together, and it will be up to you to make sure that happens and that their efforts are rewarded. You might find you need to do a lot of cajoling and keep on top of pupils (of all abilities) to get them to attend rehearsals. You might also need to do some lateral thinking; perhaps you have a talented beatboxer and an accordion player: can you find a way that they could perform together? Or how could a class of 25 six-year-olds perform a piece of music for the school assembly on the theme of 'friendship' using ukuleles and chime bars?

Qualifications

If you want to teach music in the state sector in the UK, you will have to have a recognised qualification; this is usually either a BEd degree, or a degree in your subject followed by a PGCE (Postgraduate Certificate of Education), which is a one-year full-time course (although some courses can be taken part time over a longer period). Your first year teaching following a PGCE is then as an NQT (newly qualified teacher); when this is complete you are fully qualified. In some cases, you can train while working, on the GTP (graduate training programme), but places on this scheme are not common, and are more likely to be found in subjects with shortages of teachers (such as science).

If you want to teach music in the secondary sector, your first degree will need to have been music. A good deal of performance experience is also very useful, as the curriculum up to GCSE level is very practically based. For the primary sector, a degree in music is not so vital but you will need to be able to demonstrate a good all-round musical knowledge. Practical skills such as playing the piano or guitar are also very useful, as is the ability to arrange music for different groups of musicians.

How do I get started?

If you know that you want to teach in primary schools, with music as your specialism, you could study for a BEd at university, or you could go on and do your PGCE after you have done a degree in any subject, as long as you have strong music skills. You can also come back to do a PGCE at any point after you have done your degree – some people come to teaching later in life after having followed a different career path for a while.

For secondary teaching, you will need to first take a degree in music, then go on to do your PGCE. It is possible to take a BEd course specialising in teaching music that will lead towards a career in the secondary sector, but there aren't many of these courses around.

Once you are on your PGCE course, the tutors will be helping you look for that important first job; the *Times Educational Supplement* is a good first port of call, and there are other sources of advertisements listed on the website.

ALISON HOPPER

JOB TITLE
Primary school music subject leader.

JOB DESCRIPTION
I oversee the curriculum music teaching for children aged 4–11, by monitoring planning and managing resources. I also liaise with extracurricular music providers, run lunchtime music clubs (Glee Choir and Rock Band at the moment) and coordinate the music used in assembly.

IS THIS JOB FULL-TIME?
Part time; I also have a non-musical part-time lecturing post.

WHAT WAS YOUR ROUTE TO THIS JOB?
I took a music degree, then specialised in music for my PGCE. I then moved away from music specialism into maths (they say they go together), but having returned to the classroom part time, I have picked up music again as it is a friendly subject for a part-time teacher to lead.

BEST BIT?
Being able to introduce children to the joys of different eras and styles of music – it can be a real awe-and-wonder subject.

WORST BIT?
It is often the subject which gets dropped as time gets tight in the week. It's sometimes hard to overcome the time and money constraints.

WHAT PERSONAL QUALITIES DO YOU THINK YOU HAVE THAT HELP IN YOUR JOB?
Confidence – I'm happy to stand up and sing or play in front of 300 children!
Ambition – I have high expectations of the capabilities of children aged 4–11.
Inclusivity – I believe that any child who wants to sing and play should have the chance to do so.

WHAT PRACTICAL ADVICE WOULD YOU GIVE TO SOMEONE WHO WANTED YOUR JOB?
Keep your keyboard skills honed, or find a keen piano player on the staff!

INSTRUMENTAL/SINGING TEACHING

About the job
If you want to teach your instrument(s) or singing, there are opportunities to do that all over the country. Most secondary schools (and some primary ones) have peripatetic music teachers who come in for a day or half-day every week and teach pupils individually or in small groups. For state schools, these teachers are often organised by the regional council's music providers (music hubs), and they travel round going to a different school each day (or sometimes two in the same day). Otherwise, people teach privately from their own home (or visiting the pupils' homes), recruiting pupils by advertising or word of mouth. Some people spend part of the week working in schools and take private pupils at home as well; others concentrate exclusively on one or the other.

It will be easier to fill your pupil list if you teach a popular instrument such as the guitar or piano. If you teach something a little less widespread (such as the bassoon or the lute) you will probably need to diversify to make a living. Some people teach their main study to a higher level and take on beginners on their other instrument(s), passing them on to another teacher when they reach a certain level.

As a private teacher you are free to create your own terms and conditions, but lessons usually range from half an hour (for beginners or children) up to an hour for more advanced pupils. You will set your own rates; it is worth asking around to find out what the 'going rate' is in your area. Bear in mind that you will be a self-employed worker so will be responsible for paying your own tax and National Insurance (make sure you factor that in to your income and expenditure calculations); you will also have to consider the fact that you won't have sick pay or holiday pay – and many people don't expect to have lessons outside of the school holidays. You might also have to consider aspects such as liability insurance and child protection. You can find some helpful links on the website with more information about these issues.

Qualifications
You will need to be accomplished technically in the instrument you are teaching. For teaching more advanced pupils in some areas, such as classical orchestral instruments or voice, this will mean that you should have been trained to conservatoire level or equivalent. For some genres that isn't the case – rock guitar, for example, or folk fiddle – but you will

be expected to be technically very strong and you will need to maintain that level of performing ability. London-based flautist and teacher Ruth Ballantyne advises: 'aim to get better at your instrument, even if only a little, every day.'

There are various teaching diplomas for musicians offered by the practical examination boards (such as the ABRSM or Trinity College London), as well as external qualifications offered by some of the conservatoires.

You might find, if you are teaching an instrument that traditionally needs accompaniment, or voice, that keyboard skills will come in very useful, as pupils will very often need someone to play with them.

How do I get started?
This is a job you will learn partly by doing, so a good place to start is to offer to give a few lessons to family or friends for free, so you get used to what it feels like to be in the teaching role. Some conservatoires have schemes that link their students with people looking for instrumental lessons, so you can start to gain experience while still learning yourself.

Get in touch with your local county or borough's music service to see what their criteria are for teachers they employ, and whether they might have vacancies for your instrument/voice. This will give you some sort of idea about the experience you need to be acquiring.

Other teaching opportunities
Teachers are needed also in further and higher education – universities and colleges. To teach on a university music degree, you will probably have come up through academia (have achieved or be working towards a PhD in an area of music such as analysis, composition or musicology). To teach on one of the more practical courses, such as at a conservatoire or a college of popular music, you will have to have a great deal of experience yourself of a career as a performer, producer, record industry professional and so on.

There are an increasing number of groups around the country for adults or children making music together, such as the popular Rock Choir franchise for adults or the Saturday musical theatre groups such as Stagecoach for children. There is nothing to stop an enterprising teacher creating a learning group for any type of music if there is local demand – often all it will take is the hire of a suitable venue and a lot of infectious enthusiasm.

See the Rhinegold Education website for more useful information on how to get a new group off the ground.

There are also franchises for groups that work with pre-school children, or parents and babies; some of these might offer training to new teachers wanting to lead groups. There are learning systems that work particularly well with younger children such as the Kodály or Dalcroze technique (special methods developed to help teach young children about music), and there are training systems in place for anyone wanting to teach these.

For teachers with a wealth of experience behind them, there are also opportunities to become examiners for the boards that administer the main practical music examinations (such as the ABRSM or Trinity College London), or examiners for GCSE and A levels. These roles will be part-time and will typically involve a few days' intensive work at a time, in an area away from home. But they could be a rewarding occupation alongside other sporadic employments such as performing, or for those who are semi-retired or similar.

MUSIC THERAPY

About the job
Music therapists aren't actually teachers, but they do use music to help to make a difference in people's lives. According to the British Association for Music Therapy:

> Music therapy uses [the emotional aspects of music] and the musical components of rhythm, melody and tonality to provide a means of relating within a therapeutic relationship. In music therapy, people work with a wide range of accessible instruments and their voices to create a musical language which reflects their emotional and physical condition; this enables them to build connections with their inner selves and with others around them. (www.bamt.org)

The role of music therapist usually falls within the health sector, and therapists might find work within the NHS, or for charitable groups and organisations.

There are a number of personality traits that are important to work as any kind of therapist: you need to be a calm, open and empathetic person (being able to see something from other people's point of view); you need to be able to accept people for who they are and to get on with them, whatever their background, making them feel comfortable in your company; you need to be fairly unshakable and very tolerant; most of all, you need to care about other people and want to help them. In addition to all of this, as a music therapist you need to be a very capable practical musician. It is a lot to ask of someone, to have all of these qualities, but for the right person, work as a music therapist can be enormously rewarding on a personal level.

Qualifications

Music therapists are expected to have a very high standard of musicianship, so you will need to have graduated from a three-year course at a conservatoire or have a degree in music. Other degree subjects, such as psychology or education, might be acceptable, but you would have to be able to show through other means that you have the necessary musicianship (such as a diploma-level performance qualification). You would then need to follow one of the postgraduate (Masters level) music therapy courses. Once you are qualified as a music therapist, you would need to be registered with the Health Professions Council.

How do I get started?

As well as following the education route outlined above, there are things you can do to help to prove to a potential employer (and to yourself!) that you can do this work. It would be a good idea to get some experience in working in a care-giving environment, and there are many organisations who would welcome volunteers. You could use a website such as www.do-it.org.uk to find out about volunteering opportunities in your area working with children or adults with learning difficulties or with elderly people, for example. There are also opportunities to volunteer in supporting roles to music therapists – for example, see the work of Music as Therapy (www.musicastherapy.org).

TINA WARNOCK

JOB TITLE
HCPC registered music therapist (freelance) and head of service at Belltree Music Therapy Centre.

JOB DESCRIPTION
I use musical improvisation to build connections with people who find it hard to communicate verbally. This might be due to autism, a physical or learning disability, illness, trauma, brain injury, dementia or emotional distress. I also provide supervision for other music therapists and manage the service at Belltree (www.belltree.org.uk).

WHAT WAS YOUR ROUTE TO THIS JOB?
After my social psychology degree I volunteered in a special school, then got a job as a teaching assistant there, while doing a lot of singing and songwriting generally.

In my late twenties I applied and got a place on a music therapy course. After qualifying I worked for the NHS as a music therapist for six years, then started my own social enterprise in my local area.

BEST BIT?
Feeling inspired by the quality of communication I can experience with people who are often emotionally isolated; working in a field I feel passionate about and that uses my musical skills; being able to decide where I work and when, to fit in with family commitments.

WORST BIT?
The lack of job security; having to explain what I do frequently, as people are often not familiar with music therapy.

WHAT PERSONAL QUALITIES DO YOU THINK YOU HAVE THAT HELP IN YOUR JOB?
A flexible non-judgemental approach to people; being a good listener; using my initiative to keep the work coming.

WHAT PRACTICAL ADVICE WOULD YOU GIVE TO SOMEONE WHO WANTED YOUR JOB?
You need to be very proactive. Make sure you have explored your own musicianship extensively before training to be a therapist. Don't rush into it – enjoy reading and learning about it before you commit to the training.

4. Professional organisations and music charities

PROFESSIONAL ORGANISATIONS

About the job

There are professional organisations all over the country that support the work that musicians do in all its varieties. For example, the Arts Councils of England, Wales and Northern Ireland (and the Scottish equivalent, Creative Scotland) help to provide funding for musicians to perform and work as educators, bringing music to communities across the UK. The Performing Right Society (PRS for Music) and the Mechanical-Copyright Protection Society (MCPS) work to ensure that musicians are paid the money they are due from the use of their music, whether it is being performed live or in recorded form. There are also organisations that work with specific groups – for example, the National Association for Music Educators (NAME*), the Schools Music Association (SMA) and the Music Education Council (MEC) work with people teaching music; the Federation of Music Services (FMS) links and supports the regional groups all over the country who provide music services to young people (such as providing music lessons in schools, or running county youth orchestras); the Music Publishers' Association (MPA) works to support those who publish music and books about music; and the organisation Sound Sense works to support community music groups across the country.

These organisations, and others like them, need staff who know about music but who can also bring other skills to help in the running of an organisation – administrative, financial, negotiating and legal skills are

---

*NAME, which serves the music education community, and the FMS, which supports music services, are – at the time going to press – in talks to merge into one unified body to support the whole sector.

BINDU PAUL

JOB TITLE
Live performance and teaching officer,
Musicians' Union (MU).

JOB DESCRIPTION
I provide organisational and administrative support
to the national organiser and I help deliver the MU strategy on live performance
and teaching. I have recently been speaking to students at conservatoires about
the pitfalls of the music industry and how the MU can help. I have also spoken
to members about the teaching section.

WHAT WAS YOUR ROUTE TO THIS JOB?
I started just over three years ago, following a degree in politics. I was the
regional administrator for the Wales and Southwest region based in Cardiff, then
in 2010 I covered a maternity post in the London office before taking up my new
role of live performance and teaching officer in March 2011.

BEST BIT?
Helping and advising people when they are in a difficult situation. Being involved
with great projects that help people who work in music education.

WORST BIT?
Seeing spending cuts affecting our members and their careers.

WHAT PERSONAL QUALITIES DO YOU THINK YOU HAVE THAT HELP IN YOUR JOB?
I have had some great experience in advising people and giving the best
knowledge of the union and how we can help them. I feel like I can deliver a
good presentation. I am approachable and friendly and I think my best quality
is that I will always try to do the best I can to help people with their problem. I
think I have been trained well to do this by working for the union.

**WHAT PRACTICAL ADVICE WOULD YOU GIVE TO
SOMEONE WHO WANTED YOUR JOB?**
Being involved and interested in trade-union issues, and music-education
knowledge would also be useful. If you are willing to work hard and do a variety
of jobs and tasks, you will be well equipped for this job. Interpersonal skills,
being confident and using your initiative will also help.

all useful in this area. These jobs are probably not glamorous, but form a vital support to music-making and education in the UK. Many of the organisations are small and funding is often tight, so versatility (being able to lend your hand to a number of different tasks) would probably also be very useful.

Qualifications

This is the sort of role you could come at from a number of different directions. A degree in music might be a good starting point, if you could supplement it with other useful training (such as secretarial skills or book-keeping). Or you could come from a background in a completely different area (perhaps as an administrator, lawyer or accountant), and back that up with musical knowledge gained in your spare time. If you have a background as a music teacher, for example, that would be useful for going to work for one of the organisations that support music education.

How do I get started?

If you think this is an area in which you'd like to work, start as soon as you can to widen your skills base. If you are a music student, for example, temping work in an office during your college holidays will be very useful experience to become accustomed to office procedures, as would classes in accountancy/book-keeping, or an introduction to law. If you are a student in a different subject, do all you can to widen your musical knowledge by keeping up to date with developments in your area through specialist magazines or on the internet, or by taking part as a performer. If you think something like the Musicians' Union will be of interest to you, get involved with local politics or the Students' Union – all of this can be excellent experience. As always, any volunteering work you can have on your CV for these types of organisations (or related ones) will stand you in very good stead.

MUSIC CHARITIES

About the job

There are a number of organisations in the UK who operate as charities connected to music, each in a particular field. For example, the charity Youth Music works to use music 'to transform the lives of disadvantaged children and young people'; the Musicians Benevolent Fund and the Royal Society of Musicians exist to give support to musicians who have a financial crisis or during old age; Nordoff Robbins provides music therapy and related services to help vulnerable adults and children. There are many more music-related charities across the country, of varying sizes.

Because charities, of course, depend on donations and grants to do their work, there won't be much money available to pay staff so wages won't be high, and often employees will be needed to turn their hand to whatever needs doing for the organisation. But many people get great personal satisfaction from working in a role that does a lot to help others.

Qualifications
The skills and attributes needed to work for one of the music charities are very similar to those needed by the professional organisations: a love for and knowledge of music coupled with practical administrative, financial, negotiating and/or legal skills. In addition, though, you will need to have an understanding of the particular aims of the charity, and be sympathetic to them. Adaptability is important as well – being able to help out with whatever needs doing at the time.

How do I get started?
Some people find their way into working for a charity because they are very interested in a particular field. If, for example, you are a passionate supporter of the importance of music in the lives of the under-fives, then it would seem natural to be drawn to a charity that supports that work. Jobs in this sector might not be very plentiful, as there is not a lot of money to go round, but look out for advertisements for entry-level positions such as administrative assistants. You will need to be able to demonstrate your adaptability (so see the comments about broadening your skills base in the professional organisations section on page 39), but more importantly to show a commitment to the cause(s) of the charity. Many of these charities will rely a great deal on voluntary workers, so take every opportunity to volunteer yourself. It doesn't necessarily have to be volunteering for the organisation where you are applying for a job, but it will show that you understand the practicalities of working with volunteers and that you believe in what they are trying to do.

ARTS ADMINISTRATION, MANAGEMENT AND PROMOTION

Last time you went to a festival or a concert or gig, did you think about how it came to happen? For any event to take place there is an enormous number of jobs that need to be done. For a big event, such as Glastonbury, there will be a whole army of people helping to make it happen; for a small event, like a live gig in the back room of a pub, there might only be one or two people doing everything. But if you are an organised and energetic person, arts administration or management might be the career for you.

Take a concert series or festival, for example. Someone has to plan the event (who will be performing what), work out the budgeting and sponsorship, and book the artists for the right price (some might be booked up years ahead; others might only agree to perform if they are headlining; others might be keen but will have to find a way to get back from East Asia the day before). Then there will be venues to organise and book, a marketing campaign to implement and booking systems to put in place – all timed so that enough people know about the event and can book easily to make sure there is the maximum possible income from ticket sales. For the event itself there might be programmes to organise and there will definitely be front of house to consider (from someone to take the tickets and sell the programmes for a little classical concert, to fencing and security teams for large festivals). Someone will need to be there to oversee things on the day itself, as well as looking after the artists who are performing and making sure they have everything they need – perhaps a glass of water on stage or a whole PA system and light show. Finally, there will be tidying up to do after any event, budgets to finalise and then hopefully good reviews to collect, ready to show the sponsors for the next year's event. That is an enormous amount of work and some of the bigger events can keep a whole team of people in full-time employment.

From the other side of things, there are also people involved behind the scenes helping the performers to organise their lives. Many performers are either too busy to organise things for themselves, or prefer to concentrate on the musical side of the job and leave the business organisation to other people. So this could involve coordinating bookings, negotiating (and chasing) payments, organising travel and running a publicity campaign.

With such an enormous variety of work going on out of sight, there are all sorts of opportunities for specialising in one area or another. For example, if you are good with figures or perhaps have a background in accountancy then there could be job opportunities in the budgeting, sponsorship or grant-allocating areas. Or perhaps with training in marketing and/or sales, a dedicated PR position for an organisation, venue or artist could be the job for you. Anyone hoping to work for smaller operations, though, would do well to have some experience of all of these areas, as they may well find themselves doing a little bit of everything.

The one thing that is common to all of these roles, however, is the need to be incredibly organised. Whether you are in control of one little part of an event (such as front of house) or a whole festival, you will need to be able to keep on top of everything. It would also be very useful to be able to get on with all sorts of people and to keep calm in a crisis: for example, performers and public alike can be difficult at times, and need to be treated respectfully; it might sometimes be very important to be nice to a possible sponsor, even when you think they are behaving unreasonably.

ORCHESTRAS

About the job
A symphony orchestra can have around a hundred regular players, which is an awful lot of people to coordinate. Since many orchestral players also have other jobs (such as playing in chamber groups or teaching), they will need to have very clear information from their management about where they need to be and when for rehearsals, performances and touring, which means there are opportunities for people with a background in personnel management. In addition to the jobs involved with any artist management, such as PR and budgeting, orchestras also sometimes employ librarians to coordinate the sheet music, or specialist tour or concert managers. Most groups also now get involved in some sort of educational or outreach work as well as performing, so there is work to be done on the educational side of things. If you think you might be interested in this area, take a look at the websites of some of the larger orchestras to get an idea of the range and variety of roles within the organisation.

Qualifications
A lot will depend on what area of the organisation you would like to be involved with. For example, if you are interested in joining the marketing team then there are courses that can be followed and qualifications obtained in that discipline; the same can be said for finance and budgeting. First-hand knowledge of what an orchestra is and does will be invaluable as well. For example, if you are the person responsible for booking the extra players needed for a performance of Messiaen's *Turangalîla Symphony*, you'll need to know that it needs an ondes Martenot player (as well as

MARIE-SOPHIE WILLIS

JOB TITLE
Chief executive of The Sixteen (a leading professional choir and instrument ensemble).

JOB DESCRIPTION
Managing the business, operations and artistic planning for the group.

WHAT WAS YOUR ROUTE TO THIS JOB?
I started by gaining a degree in music at Oxford and then an MA in arts administration. I then worked at the Royal Opera House as editorial assistant, the English National Opera as casting and auditions coordinator, Aldeburgh Music as artistic administrator and the Monteverdi Choir and Orchestra as artistic and development planner.

I have had a variety of different jobs which have each taught me very different things. The varied experiences within both small and large organisations have allowed me to get a real overview of the many different aspects involved with running a small organisation.

BEST BIT?
The most satisfying part of the job for me is both the artistic planning and ensuring the business side is all working! The challenge each season is both to fill the diary and provide work for our performers, but also to develop relationships with new promoters and venues, and to expand The Sixteen's foothold in various territories.

WORST BIT?
Dealing with the everyday admin – finances, insurance, personnel, etc.

WHAT PERSONAL QUALITIES DO YOU THINK YOU HAVE THAT HELP IN YOUR JOB?
I think it is fairly essential to be able to get on with a wide variety of people at different levels. In a role such as this you are dealing with many different types of people – performers, donors and supporters, promoters, agents, etc. Flexibility is also important; plans change all the time and it is good to try to have a philosophical attitude to that, otherwise stress can set in! Communication and negotiation skills are also key to the role. And a sense of humour helps ... especially in a small team where it is fairly crucial that everyone gels. Most people entering the arts profession have different motivations from people entering

a career in, say, banking. We all tend to share the same goal and vision and are (hopefully!) working in the environment because we have a similar passion for the music and love of the artform.

WHAT PRACTICAL ADVICE WOULD YOU GIVE TO SOMEONE WHO WANTED YOUR JOB?
Get as much different experience as possible – in other words, don't just have a career path that focuses on one niche. Try and have jobs along the way that will give you a chance to work in different areas. A stint in artistic planning is helpful as it gives such a good experience of pulling together concerts, dealing with different personalities, budgeting and negotiating; but it is also useful at some point to have a job involving fundraising as that is often a big part of a CEO/general manager job. Also, try and work in both a small and large company as the two will give you very useful and different experiences – in a small company it is easier to get an overview of the different departments.

what an ondes Martenot is, and how to go about finding someone that can play one!). So a music degree isn't necessarily essential, but will be a very good starting point. If you have had experience in playing in your school or youth orchestra, or orchestra at college, this will also be helpful.

How do I get started?
Experience in the types of work needed around orchestras can usefully be gained at college, helping to organise student orchestras or other amateur groups. Some of the larger orchestras also run internship schemes, so you might be able to get an unpaid work placement to enhance your CV. You will then need to keep an eye on the websites for the various orchestras to look out for that vital first job that can help you get your foot in the door.

OPERA COMPANIES

About the job
As if the logistics of an orchestra weren't complicated enough, an opera company will also employ a chorus and soloists, and all the backstage people who help any theatrical production come alive (costume, make-up, lighting, stage management, etc.). From the musical side of things, the

roles are very similar, although anyone involved with touring or scheduling will have more things to consider (such as getting sets assembled in each venue on a tour, or organising the singers to come for costume fittings).

FESTIVALS

About the job
As described in the introduction to this chapter, there is an enormous variety of roles involved in getting a festival off the ground. As well as the high-profile rock festivals such as Glastonbury, Reading or Green Man, there are folk festivals like those at Cambridge or Sidmouth, classical festivals such as the BBC Proms, mixed-genre festivals like Edinburgh and all sorts of smaller-scale festivals going on all over the country, catering for all tastes.

Working for one of the bigger festivals could mean a full-time job in a very specific role (such as marketing or fundraising manager), whereas working for a smaller one might mean taking on a lot of different roles. For example, Emma Cross, administrator of Bath's Mozartfest and Bachfest, says about her responsibilities: 'Once the artists have been chosen, I then make the concert happen – contracting, venue, lighting, staffing, staging, instruments, hotels, etc.'.

Qualifications
You will need a lot of energy and organisational skills, and you will need to have a good knowledge of the music that you will be promoting. It is also very important to be good with people. You will very probably be working as part of a team, so being able to coordinate with other people and get the job done under pressure is very important; so too is being able to deal diplomatically with the audience member who has a complaint or the rock star diva who insists on a bubble machine in their dressing room.

How do I get started?
Once again, experience is very important, and anything you can do at school or college to help run events will be very useful. A lot of festivals rely on volunteers to act as stewards or to help run events. While many people use this as a good way of getting to see the performances for free, it can also be something that will show your dedication to gaining experience in the right sort of roles.

LINDSEY DEAR

JOB TITLE
General manager of the City of London Festival

JOB DESCRIPTION
I am responsible for the implementation and successful operational delivery of an annual multi-arts festival, as well as other activity undertaken by the organisation throughout the year. I line-manage the staff team (full- and part-time staff, volunteer interns, freelance project staff, animateurs and technicians on contract) and have overall responsibility for all festival staff including more than 100 volunteers. I set budgets for all projects, and manage the financial and administrative resource for the festival programme, including the negotiation of artist contracts and fundraising. I am also responsible for the smooth running of the office and other working environments, and for ensuring that effective systems and policies are in place.

WHAT WAS YOUR ROUTE TO THIS JOB?
As a passionate amateur musician, I became interested in event management as a teenager, and held various committee posts with student choirs and orchestras through school and university where I did a BA in English literature. After graduation, I worked in radio, first in programme-making and then within an in-house events team. I gained knowledge and experience, and was promoted through the ranks before leaving to pursue a less commercially focused career in the arts. I took a role with a festival, and found that I very much enjoyed the nature of the work. I have now worked at a senior management level within the festival sector for ten years.

BEST BIT?
I really enjoy working creatively within a very practical framework, and being able to see a project through from beginning to end, from the barest sketch of a creative idea on the back of an envelope to the performance itself.

An exciting and motivating element of my work is facilitating and managing artistic collaborations: working with composers, musicians, writers, visual artists, choreographers, dancers and film-makers. Much of my work involves interpreting the creative aims of others, which can be a privilege.

WORST BIT?
The constant struggle for economic sustainability. The enormous efforts and disappointments of fundraising – particularly in the current depressed financial climate – is my least favourite aspect of my job. It also means that I frequently have to be the person that says 'no' to what I know would be exciting, creative, relevant, interesting projects, if only we could find the money to make them happen. For every critical success, there are another twenty great ideas lying in a drawer.

WHAT PERSONAL QUALITIES DO YOU THINK YOU HAVE THAT HELP IN YOUR JOB?
I think that my combination of nit-pickingly annoying attention to detail, strong organisation and communication skills and a huge passion for the arts have helped me develop my career.

WHAT PRACTICAL ADVICE WOULD YOU GIVE TO SOMEONE WHO WANTED YOUR JOB?
Get involved! While there are now a plethora of event/festival management degree courses on offer, the academic opportunity they offer should not be a substitute for real, hands-on experience. Experience doesn't necessarily have to be in a professional context – an ongoing voluntary role with your local community arts organisation, for example, will show a potential employer that you have both passion and commitment.

CONCERT PROMOTER

About this job
A concert promoter will liaise between artists (and their agents) and venues to put on a concert, or series of concerts. They will not be tied to any one venue or any one artist, but will promote concerts as an entrepreneurial activity. To begin with, the promoter will need to secure financial backing for the event, either by finding backers or by putting up the money themselves. They will then need to secure the right venue and the right artist(s) at the right price, as well as organise all the other aspects of the event, which could include contracts, advertising and publicity, ticketing, running the show, technical liaison, and so on. The aim of all of this will be to make money so that the backer sees a good return on his or her investment.

Anyone wanting to work as a concert promoter will need to be entrepreneurial, imaginative (able to see what sort of event is going to be popular), hard-working and business savvy. One thing worth remembering is that if an event isn't a success, it is often the promoter who won't be paid (or who, worse still, will be liable for any debts). Good initial experience would be to put on an event at your local pub, or for a student venue. You could also consider helping a charity to put on a fundraiser as a way of gaining some experience. There are a number of companies that specialise in concert promotion, and an entry-level position in one of these could be a good way to get started.

VENUES

Performances take place in all sorts of venues, from the O2 arena to the local church hall, and all of these places will need backroom support of one kind or another. Many of the available roles will be similar to those working for an orchestra, opera company or festival, mentioned above. Look at the websites for the sorts of venues where your genre of music is played to get an idea of the work opportunities that could be available there. And, as with the other kinds of administration roles, experience is going to be a key aspect to getting that first job so look out for chances to work as a volunteer or intern.

ARTIST MANAGEMENT

About the job
While some musicians prefer to manage their own affairs, most employ a manager to help with the business side of things. A large number of performers also use an agent, who may or may not be the same person as their manager, to promote them to bookers and recording companies, and to manage their diaries. In addition, a number of people use independent public relations (PR) consultants to help them to market themselves. A good manager will also find gigs that will advance their artists' careers, put them in touch with other musicians, writers and so on who they think will work well together, as well as organise all other aspects such as tours, negotiations to get a record deal, and so on.

ALAN EDWARDS

JOB TITLE
CEO of an entertainment PR company.

JOB DESCRIPTION
I deal with every aspect of running a PR company from budgets to front-line PR.

WHAT WAS YOUR ROUTE TO THIS JOB?
I started at the bottom and worked up. My first job was as a messenger, then I moved to ad sales, became a freelance reviewer and PR assistant, and then a PR. I then left employment and formed my own publicity company.

BEST BIT?
Variety. The unpredictability means that each week is an adventure! I have met many fascinating people from all walks of life imaginable.

WORST BIT?
The unpredictability ... sometimes I wish I had gone for the nine-to-five option! Seriously though – entertainment PR is nowhere near as well paid as people imagine.

WHAT PERSONAL QUALITIES DO YOU THINK YOU HAVE THAT HELP IN YOUR JOB?
It is vital to like the people you are pitching stories to (journalists) and to have an appreciation of their profession. The ability to get on with people whatever their background or status is also very helpful.

It is important to be able to think creatively to help advise clients about new ways of getting their message across. Physical and mental stamina, and a thickish skin also help!

WHAT PRACTICAL ADVICE WOULD YOU GIVE TO SOMEONE WHO WANTED YOUR JOB?
Study the media and try to visualise where it's going and how it will evolve. Start practising your own PR campaigns and figure out where potential clients might get best coverage. Try to get practical experience and begin to build up your own network of contacts. Do as much of your own research as possible.

Qualifications

As well as a good general knowledge of music, and a passionate belief in their artists, a manager needs a whole raft of business skills, including financial, administrative, marketing and negotiation skills. There are a number of dedicated courses in music management, such as those run by the Music Managers Forum.

How do I get started?

Jon Webster, of the Music Managers Forum, advises: 'Find a great act! Have passion. Share your artists' vision … get your hands dirty and learn as you go along.'

5. Publishing

Before the advent of affordable recording media (beginning with 78rpm vinyl records, through LPs, cassette tapes, CDs into MP3s), popular songs were circulated as sheet music, which many people would play on their piano at home. At this time, music publishers became one of the most important sectors of the music industry. The same is true today, but actually physically publishing sheet music is only one part of what they do. Composers, then and now, sign with music publishers, who protect the rights to their compositions, collect royalties that are due (although of course artists can join PRS for Music without being signed to a publisher), and promote their use – both by recording artists, and in film and television – as well as, of course, publishing them as sheet music and increasingly in electronic form. Music publishers' A&R (artist and repertoire) professionals will often also help with a composer's development, perhaps introducing them to co-writers or making suggestions as to a niche they can fill.

Singer-songwriters will aim to sign with both a record company and a music publisher – one to protect and promote their performances (recordings), and the other to do the same for their compositions (the actual songs and lyrics).

The roles within the music publishing industry are quite varied and there are opportunities for all sorts of personality types. Gregarious people who enjoy team-working might find they would like a role in A&R, which involves working with all sorts of different people, whereas those who prefer an office-based existence might be happier in something like accounts and royalties, or an editorial role.

SYNCH

About the job
'Synch' is short for 'synchronisation', and is the department of the publishing company that deals with licensing compositions for use in TV, films, advertisements, video games, and so on. It used to be that a composer's recordings and sheet music were the primary source of their income, and

synch was 'secondary exploitation', but in recent years it has become more and more a platform on which an artist's career can be launched.

The synch professionals will work with almost all areas of the music publishing and recording industry. They need to have their fingers on the pulse, so they're aware of the hot new bands and artists that are up and coming. They need to have an extensive knowledge of music in general (and a specialist knowledge of one or more particular area(s) would be helpful) so that they know what sounds might be available when they are working with ad agencies or production companies. They need to have an understanding of rights, royalties and the law so that they can negotiate the best deal for their composers.

The role is a mixture of 'hard' sales (for example, going to visit production companies with a showreel of compositions in order to persuade them to use the music), and negotiation and creative skills (working closely with production companies to help them to find the music that creates just the effect they are looking for).

Qualifications

As the synch department liaises with so many different departments across the industry, there is no one particular qualification that will be needed. The most important requirement is a passion for music – of any kind and all kinds. A synch professional's best asset is a gut feeling for what music will work in any particular scenario. Communication skills are vital, both for working with the team and for liaising with the various external contacts. A good technical and musical knowledge is also important.

People come into a synch role from all sorts of different backgrounds, some from a creative side (perhaps from an advertising agency or TV production company), some from other areas of the music industry, some from a legal or licensing background, some from broadcasters such as the BBC, and so on.

How do I get started?

You might choose to follow a course in the music business, or a short course in music industry practices, such as those run by the Music Publishers Association (MPA). An entry-level job (such as administrative assistant, or any junior role) in any related industry would be a good first step – this could include advertising agencies, production companies, broadcasters, video games companies, organisations that produce corporate videos, artist management companies, and so on. Aim to use these roles to build up your overall general knowledge of the industry, how it fits together and how music is dealt with and treated from one type of organisation to the next.

A&R

About the job
A&R stands for artists and repertoire, and this is the department that finds and nurtures talent for the publishers. There could be a number of roles within the department (depending on the size of the organisation), and between them they might discover and sign new talent, help the songwriters to develop their material, liaise with their counterparts in A&R departments in recording companies to link songwriters and performers together, and work with the songwriter on developing their career. They might thus work with the synch, marketing, licensing and editorial/ production departments, as well as acting as talent scouts for the publisher.

Qualifications
As with the jobs in the synch department, there is no one particular route into A&R. There are a number of attributes, though, that could help in this role: a great overall knowledge of the music business and what is hot at any particular time (to be able to see which niche any particular composer might fill); great people skills (to make and maintain contacts in all areas of the publishing and recording industries); imagination and creativity (to be able to envisage where a composer might go next, and to suggest ways for them to develop and/or branch out); and a good technical musical knowledge (to be able to advise on the nuts and bolts of songwriting). This last point isn't always seen as a prerequisite for A&R executives, but it is something that is appreciated by many composers.

How do I get started?
Since you will need contacts and experience for this role, anything that can get those for you will be a good first step. Internship roles in music publishers and related businesses are of course valuable, but so is any kind of experience with synch agencies, recording companies, video/film pro-duction companies, and so on. Work hard to develop your own knowledge of songwriting and of the current music scene, do as much networking as you can, and look for entry-level positions (such as administration assistant) in publishing or a related industry for your first step on the ladder.

RIGHTS, LICENSING, ACCOUNTS AND ROYALTIES

About the job
There are various departments within music publishers who will handle the important legal and financial aspects of the organisation. How the work is distributed between the departments, and what they are called, will vary from one organisation to another, but on the legal side they will cover contracting (both between the artist and the organisation, and with external organisations such as TV companies), and on the financial side they will deal with the very important task of collecting royalties due and making sure these are distributed to the artists. The licensing (or copyright) department will deal with requests from third parties to use songs by composers managed by the publisher, but also do all the checking to ensure that the material included in any of the organisation's publications (both hard copy and digital) is properly credited and paid for.

Qualifications
Legal and/or financial qualifications (e.g. a degree in law, for working in the licensing department) would be helpful, although not compulsory, for these sorts of roles. Some people do follow this route after taking a degree in music, but often a good self-taught knowledge of, and interest in, music will be enough. Most important for these vital jobs are diligence and attention to detail – a lot of the work will be very meticulous and there is little room for error. For those roles within the departments that deal with negotiating contracts, excellent interpersonal skills are needed in order to agree on the best deal for the organisation and the individual composer.

How do I get started?
If you know that you will be interested in working in this sort of area, you might perhaps already be working towards a qualification in a related subject (e.g. law, music). It will do you good, as well, to do your research to develop your knowledge about the music industry as a whole. Work experience and/or internships in a department related to rights, licensing or royalties would be advantageous. You will then need to look for an administrative or assistant role as your first paid position.

PRODUCTION AND EDITORIAL

As well as representing and promoting composers and their works, the music publishing sector in the UK produces magazines (both in print and online), and books about music from the general to the specialised, sheet music and music educational material. Increasingly, also, they are involved with the fast-growing area of digital publishing (e-books, and so on). All of these need staff with specialised music knowledge on top of their skills as editors, typesetters, or whatever their main job is.

About the job

The editorial staff of a publisher organise all aspects of production, from concept development and author commissioning to having the material typeset, printed and distributed. It is the editors who check all the writing or music arrangement to make sure it fits the brief, flows well and is free from errors. There is a team of people involved in all of this, so being able to work well with others is an important part of the job. It is also quite varied, so the ability to multitask is very useful.

Editors need to have an extremely good eye for detail. These are the people who will notice that Jimi Hendrix's birthdate has been given as 1942 in Chapter 2 but 1943 in Chapter 8, or that the chord symbol gives Em^9 but the chord on the score is an Em^7. They will be able to improve the structure of a piece of writing to make it flow more logically, or adapt the writing to make the language more appropriate for different markets.

Schedules are vitally important in publishing – there are lots of people involved in the process, so if one person is late completing their stage it has implications for everyone else further down the line. To be in control of this, you need to be extremely organised and to be able to keep the long-term ramifications in mind while still dealing with all the tiny details. As Tom Farncombe, managing editor at Music Sales (one of the world's largest music publishers), puts it: 'You need to be meticulously concerned with detail on one hand while keeping abreast of the bigger picture at the same time'.

The commissioning editor is the person who decides what book needs to be written, and finds the right people to write it, sometimes getting other people on board such as illustrators or music arrangers as well. A commissioning editor is usually someone with a good deal of experience in all areas of the publishing industry, gained through working in lots of other different roles. It is essential to this role not only that you know the publishing industry very well but also that you know all about the market (i.e. your potential customers), because it's important to be able to see where the gaps are and what new products could fill them.

CHRIS CHARLESWORTH

JOB TITLE
Editor-in-chief, Omnibus Press.

JOB DESCRIPTION
I am responsible for the commissioning and editing of about 30-35 books a year, all of them relating to music, principally rock and pop. I have one co-editor who works largely on the commissioning side while I concentrate on the editorial side but we share duties. If the work load becomes too onerous we commission freelance editors to help. I liaise with authors while the work is being done, and go through the manuscripts when they are delivered, checking for literacy and accuracy. I write or edit cover copy, oversee photo research, liaise with others over cover photos and design, and deal with proofing. I have overall responsibility for each book until it is sent to print. I also contribute to sheet music books which require text of a biographical nature.

WHAT WAS YOUR ROUTE TO THIS JOB?
After I left school I became a trainee journalist on a local weekly newspaper, combining this with a college course. I began writing about pop music for two provincial daily papers, then joined the staff of Melody Maker, then the UK's best-selling weekly music paper, for which I worked throughout the 1970s. During this period I interviewed or wrote about every major rock star of the era. After I left Melody Maker in 1977 I worked for a management company (managing The Who and others), then a record company (RCA) doing PR work. I left RCA in 1981 to become a freelance writer. I wrote eight books about music and musicians including three for Omnibus Press, whose then editor recommended me to take over his job when he left in 1983. I have been at Omnibus Press ever since, though in the late 1980s I combined this with night work as a sub-editor at the Daily Telegraph (to hone professional editing skills).

BEST BIT?
The satisfaction of seeing a book I commissioned and edited do well – in other words, get good reviews and reprint many times. This is especially the case if the book was my idea in the first place. I also take a delight in receiving a first-rate manuscript from a professional author and trying to improve it.

WORST BIT?
Chasing authors who are invariably late delivering their text; dealing with lawyers over (often groundless) complaints about libel and copyright infringements; seeing one of our books flop!

WHAT PERSONAL QUALITIES DO YOU THINK YOU HAVE THAT HELP IN YOUR JOB?
A love of books. A deep love, understanding and knowledge of popular music, from the pre-Elvis era right the way through to the present day, and a similar familiarity with the literature of pop and those who created it. As far as editing is concerned, the ability to concentrate and a broad knowledge of what constitutes literate prose. I also play the guitar and have a pretty good knowledge of the history of the instrument and the important guitar manufacturers.

WHAT PRACTICAL ADVICE WOULD YOU GIVE TO SOMEONE WHO WANTED YOUR JOB?
Read at least 50 of the best rock biographies ever published. Learn as much as you can about the history of rock and pop music. Also study and read classic fiction by noted literary authors. Read the music press. Gain a practical knowledge of the tradecraft involved in book publishing – commissioning, contracts, editorial skills, proofing, photo editing, and so on. Doing what I do is very specialist – it's no good being a good editor but knowing little about music and no good knowing a great deal about music but being unable to edit properly. It's a combination of the two that's essential.

The copy-editing and proofreading of texts (and sometimes sheet music) are often sent out of house to freelance editors, who are self-employed. Some of these professionals are music specialists (with a degree or other qualification in music), but will usually work on other kinds of texts as well.

Qualifications
Some people come into the job from a qualification in journalism (with a good level of music knowledge), but more common are those who enter the job after getting a degree in music. There are few specific editorial qualifications, although there are now a few postgraduate degrees in publishing. Acquiring proofreading and/or copy-editing skills with a respected provider such as the Publishing Training Centre or the Society for Editors and Proofreaders could be useful.

Knowing about books and scores is important, though, and a lot of that will be self-taught. As Tom Farncombe writes, 'the skills for editing sheet music and creating good editions of a song or piece of music are best developed out of a passion for scores in the first place, so you should work with printed music as much as you can: transcribing, learning about music engraving, understanding the finer points of notation and how music should be presented'.

How do I get started?
Getting the first job in publishing is the hardest part. Any experience you can get while a student (such as helping out on a student newspaper) will stand you in good stead. A number of publishers now offer opportunities for unpaid internships, and these are a first step on the ladder for those that can afford to take them up. Jenni Norey, rock and pop editor at Music Sales, writes: 'I don't think there's just one route to this job, so don't worry about having to take a set path to get here'.

Chief Operating Officer of Music Sales, Chris Butler heads up Publishing, and is also the current Chair of the Music Publisher's Association – you can read his story and his advice on getting into the music publishing industry on the Rhinegold Education website.

DIGITAL PUBLISHING

About the job
Publishing is moving very quickly into the digital realm, which means that there are new means of sharing information that are constantly evolving. It's a very exciting area of the industry to be involved with, but needs someone who has strong technical skills as well as the usual editorial and musical ones.

As this is such a new area, there are no specific qualifications that you will need to have. However, you could come to this sort of role with a background in music technology or computing. In addition, the postgraduate publishing courses are now incorporating digital publishing into their curricula, which would give you a basic grounding.

SAM HARROP

JOB TITLE
Digital content manager

JOB DESCRIPTION
I look after all content on the website sheetmusicdirect.com, such as sheet music, backing tracks and video lesson content. This includes basic editing of the scores/multimedia products before upload to the site, making sure the songs are correctly linked to our royalties system and working closely with the marketing team to create onsite promotions and features. I also keep an eye on current popular music and what our customers are looking for in order to commission new arrangements to go on the site.

In addition, I project manage a series of other digital products such as iPhone/iPad apps for musicians. Again, editing of the music content is necessary, as well as a very close eye for detail and an understanding of usability. I work closely with the design and development teams and see these projects through from conception right through to final testing before release.

WHAT WAS YOUR ROUTE TO THIS JOB?
Having graduated from university with a music degree, I was very keen to get into the world of publishing. I responded to an advert for a job as music editor for Music Sales and started working in the print editorial team in the London office. Around 18 months later, a vacancy arose in the digital team, which was an area of interest for me. I worked in this role for around 18 months and was then promoted to digital content manager.

BEST BIT?
The wide variety of projects I have to work on means I don't get bored easily. It's exciting working with new technologies and creating products which you know will be useful to musicians all around the world. For someone who loves music, it's a very rewarding position.

WORST BIT?
Although the variety is great, it's rarely possible to focus on one particular project at any one time, which can be frustrating, but it's part and parcel of the job!

WHAT PERSONAL QUALITIES DO YOU THINK YOU HAVE THAT HELP IN YOUR JOB?

The role is quite a creative one. We are constantly thinking up new ideas for apps and other projects, so creative flair is absolutely necessary. The job is very varied and usually very busy, so it's important to be able to multitask. Lastly, it's important to be diplomatic and open to other people's ideas. Working with development, marketing and design teams, there are a lot of opinions which need to be respected.

WHAT PRACTICAL ADVICE WOULD YOU GIVE TO SOMEONE WHO WANTED YOUR JOB?

Sadly, it's hard to find vacancies in digital publishing to apply for, so it may well be necessary to start working in a less exciting role in publishing and move across. Be persistent and patient, and don't be put off if you don't hear back from employers.

OTHER PUBLISHING JOBS

Music engravers or typesetters create the scores that go into music publications. These people are employed on a freelance basis; there aren't many opportunities for this sort of work in house. Whereas music used to be set by hand, these days the work is done digitally so computer literacy is necessary. Most importantly, though, a music engraver needs to have an excellent musical knowledge combined with a good eye and creative flair.

There are opportunities within publishing companies of all kinds for people in the sales and marketing departments, and so this is also the case for music publishers. To work in marketing, people need to be creative and good communicators, and a good all-round knowledge of music would be useful in this context. If you are interested in this side of the business, the Chartered Institute of Marketing is a good place to start for information about the role and qualifications.

6. Broadcasting

Turn on your radio and flick through the stations, and you'll soon see that in the UK we have an enormous array to choose from. Some are 'talk radio', but a great number will feature music of one kind or another, from general stations playing a mixture of styles to stations dedicated to a particular genre of music, and from national stations to local. The advent of faster broadband has now also meant that music broadcasting doesn't just have to be over the analogue or digital radio – there are programmes on the internet too. There are also television programmes that feature music – whether transmitting live shows, music magazine programmes, or documentaries about artists – and so there are some opportunities available within the TV industry for people with a musical knowledge.

Jobs within the broadcasting sector are very highly sought after and it's an incredibly competitive area, both when you're getting started and when you're working your way up the ladder. Whichever area you want to work in, you will need to be extremely committed and determined. The broadcast media want people with excellent communication skills, who can work well in a team (and often independently as well), and who are dynamic and outgoing. The pressure can be immense (especially as deadlines approach, or if a programme is going out live), and you have to be someone who can keep their head and deal with any crises that might arise. If that sounds like you, broadcasting can be a hugely exciting and rewarding career.

RUNNER

About the job
This is often the first 'foot-in-the-door' post both for radio and TV. Basically, the runner does all the odd jobs that need to be done, from making the tea, to delivering scripts, welcoming guests and even driving other members of staff to where they need to be. The runner's job enables him or her to see all aspects of the TV or radio department's operations, and it's the ideal way to get a general overview of how everything works

before moving on to something else (often researcher or production assistant – see page 65).

The runner needs to have a 'can-do' attitude, as they are there to make the lives of the rest of the production team easier by taking all the 'little things' off them. It's an ideal opportunity for someone who wants to get on in the industry to make contacts and chat informally to people in all sorts of other roles, and to learn from them. The hours can be long and antisocial, and you will need to be very flexible. The pay won't be very high, but the experience will be invaluable.

Qualifications
There are no particular qualifications needed for a job as a runner (although if you are using it as a first step on the ladder, you will need to be thinking about what qualifications you would need for the next job you would want after that – see below for the other roles). However, the employer will want to see some experience on your CV, so you would do well to try to get onto one of the industry's training schemes or have an internship behind you if you can. And it goes without saying that if you want to work in music broadcasting, then you need to have a detailed knowledge of your particular genre of music (and ideally a good all-round knowledge of lots of different genres).

Since you will be expected to run a lot of errands, you will need to have a clean driving licence. You might find that other practical skills – such as training in health and safety or in first aid – will also come in useful.

How do I get started?
Get as much experience as you can – this is crucial. There are a number of community and hospital radio stations all over the country that welcome volunteers, and it's a very good way to begin to find out what is involved with the job. Some larger organisations, such as the BBC, and some national organisations run training schemes to get people started in a career in radio and TV. Runner jobs are often on a per-project basis, with a contract for a set amount of time, so you will need to keep an eye on the job advertisements the whole time, and while you are on a project be looking ahead and applying for your next one.

PRODUCTION ASSISTANT

About the job
There are various job titles that fulfil this sort of role (such as broadcast assistant, or researcher), but they all represent the next 'rung' on the ladder in the broadcast media. The assistant's job is to support the rest of the broadcast team, be they producers or presenters/DJs. This person will be involved in the planning and researching of a show, will provide administrative support to the production team, and will help out during the recording and/or broadcast. Depending on all sorts of factors (including the size of the broadcast team, the assistant's experience, and so on), they might also have a creative input to the planning (giving ideas, or following up on a particular thread) or have the opportunity to do a bit of presenting (for example, contributing to a particular slot on a radio show). In this way, it's a great learning opportunity for someone who is looking towards becoming a producer and/or presenter.

As with all of these broadcasting jobs, the assistant needs to be a team player – everyone must be working together to produce the best show they can. You will need to be highly organised and to work well under pressure, prioritising where necessary. Depending on the nature of the TV or radio show and the type of broadcaster, the job could be almost totally studio-based, or might involve some travel. It will almost definitely involve long hours, and a certain amount of unanticipated overtime.

Qualifications
You will in all probability be expected to have a degree for this sort of role. You could either go for a degree in a related subject (music, broadcast journalism, media studies), or follow up your degree in another subject with some job-specific training. You will definitely need in-depth knowledge of a particular kind of music if you want to work for a specialised music channel, or a very good general knowledge if going for something broader (such as local radio, or one of the national music stations). If you want to use this role as a stepping stone towards becoming a producer or presenter, it would be a good idea to think ahead to the qualifications you will need for that job (see below).

How do I get started?
The traditional route to this job is to undertake an internship and/or training scheme, then spend some time working as a runner (see page 63). Use these opportunities to talk to the people you are working with

and learn from them – get their tips about the jobs they are doing, listen to their stories of things that went well or badly for them and what they learnt from that. Most importantly, work hard, be willing to put yourself out, and do all you can to get on well with everyone else in the team – this is what will make you attractive to an employer.

PRESENTER/DJ

About the job
Being a radio DJ or TV presenter is a dream job for a lot of music fans. Only a few will actually make it, though, so there is a lot to do to make sure you're one of those few. As well as all the skills listed above for the other broadcasting jobs, you will need to have a big personality, a clear speaking voice and, for TV, an attractive and/or distinctive look. Presenting a programme on radio or TV could involve reading from script or improvising the spoken sections, interviewing guests, providing links and introducing recordings and sometimes reading factual sections (such as news or weather reports). In addition to your personal presenting skills and your knowledge of music, for the radio you will also need to have good technical knowledge, as it will be your responsibility to cue up music as you go along (called 'driving the desk').

There are a few downsides to the job. The hours can be long or antisocial (you might be hired to do the pre-breakfast show, for example). Don't forget, also, that you will be in the public eye – perhaps you might even become famous – and that can mean some intrusion into your private life. There's no denying, though, that this is a glamorous and exciting job, and can become well paid if you're at the top of your career.

Qualifications
You could start with a degree in music or broadcast media. Or you could start without a degree, but with great experience behind you. There are short and longer courses to help to teach presentation skills that might stand you in good stead. Some training in performing arts might also be an advantage; many TV presenters start with a course at drama school. A lot of radio DJs start off as club or mobile DJs.

How do I get started?
Experience is everything, so start by volunteering for local community, student or hospital radio. Keep your finger on the pulse of the music

BRIGGY SMALE

JOB TITLE
Radio presenter/broadcaster/voiceover artist

JOB DESCRIPTION
Formerly presenter of entertainment news on BBC
Radio 1; cultural commentator on terrestrial and
satellite TV and radio; MTV narrator.

WHAT WAS YOUR ROUTE TO THIS JOB?
After a diploma in secretarial studies, I started
work at the BBC as a personnel secretary in
corporate affairs. I moved to BBC Radio 1 Newsbeat as a production assistant and
attended various BBC training programmes so was able to progress to researcher,
broadcast journalist and senior broadcast journalist. Upon leaving the BBC,
I became programme manager at Juice 107.2 FM and set up my own media
consultancy and training company, Minxy Productions Limited.

BEST BIT?
I enjoy the variety and stimulation of having a portfolio career – my most
favourite aspect of my job is interviewing people.

WORST BIT?
Sometimes it is hard to juggle so many different jobs and having to negotiate
fees which vary considerably depending on location and the type of company
hiring me.

WHAT PERSONAL QUALITIES DO YOU THINK YOU HAVE THAT HELP IN YOUR JOB?
Communication and interpersonal skills are key elements to all of the jobs I
undertake. Confidence (or the ability to appear confident!), integrity, and being
organised and focused are also very important. Having a lot of contacts within
the various industries I work in is also very useful.

**WHAT PRACTICAL ADVICE WOULD YOU GIVE TO
SOMEONE WHO WANTED YOUR JOB?**
Be friendly, upbeat, interested and interesting. Be flexible and keen. Expect to
sometimes work for free if you feel that it may lead to future paid work. Use
every opportunity to casually network but don't be too pushy. Think of challenges
as a positive. Spread your net wide.

scene, in whichever is your chosen genre – make sure you know every-thing about what has been, as well as the up and coming talent. You will need to have a demo (no more than five minutes) to show what you can do. Follow advice about the best way to present this (see the website for some useful links, or ask tutors if you are on a music course), then get as many people in the business to listen to it as you can – ask for feedback, and use that to improve your demo. Take any opportunity to get into the industry (perhaps as a runner or assistant), and keep sharing your demo. You could set up your own website to promote yourself, perhaps even create your own online radio show or podcast; use social media to spread the word about these. Keep improving your skills and be persistent – the rest will be down to luck.

PRODUCER

About the job
The role of producer is one that is found in both TV and radio, and the jobs are similar. A programme's producer will be involved in the entire process of the show – perhaps even being the person to come up with the idea for it in the first place. He or she will plan the show, assemble the team (including production staff, presenters and so on), manage the team throughout the recording and/or broadcast period, and then follow up the audience feedback after the programme has gone out. It is a stressful but exciting job for a very organised and creative person.

Qualifications
There are a number of routes into the job, but a degree is going to be expected. If you don't take a degree in broadcast journalism or a similar discipline, there are postgraduate qualifications in radio production. There are some training schemes that have been set up for people hoping to get into the broadcast media (such as the BBC Production Training Scheme, or the Welsh Cyfle scheme).

How do I get started?
If you are determined and lucky, you might get one of the few places mentioned above on a training scheme. If not, get as much experience as you can (see suggestions above for other roles), get involved in an entry-level position (for example as a runner), and learn as you go along. At every step, ask advice from the people you are working for, and ask what you could do to improve your work.

GETHIN SCOURFIELD

JOB TITLE
Television and film producer

JOB DESCRIPTION
I produce television programmes and the occasional feature film. I have specialised in producing music-related programmes, from documentaries on individual musicians to multi-camera recording of music performances.

WHAT WAS YOUR ROUTE TO THIS JOB?
I started work in the television industry as a runner (tea boy and messenger) immediately after completing my history degree. Initially I worked on drama productions. I had always been involved in music (playing in the county youth orchestra, singing in choirs and forming a folk band in college), and in 1989 I was invited to produce an indie rock music series with three friends. This developed into a fully fledged TV production company specialising in music and arts programming – rock, world and classical. I then left to set up my own production company where I produced a music documentary feature film 'Beautiful Mistake' featuring John Cale performing with various artists, including James Dean Bradfield, Super Furry Animals and Catatonia. In 2001 I joined BBC Wales as an executive producer in the TV music department working on a range of music documentaries and performance films, from documentaries with Bryn Terfel to a film version of the popular opera 'Amahl and the Night Visitors'; from coverage of the 'Festival in the Desert' near Timbuktu in Mali to a live 'open to the public' masterclass with Barbara Bonney in Bath.

I am now freelance but still maintain a strong relationship with the music department at BBC Wales where I work as an executive producer on an occasional basis.

BEST BIT?
I have been very privileged to have had the chance to hear some fantastic music in wonderful locations. It is difficult to find fault with a job where you get a chance to meet and work with some of your heroes!

WORST BIT?
As with all jobs, there's always a down side. Dealing with the logistics can be very tiresome but probably the biggest nightmare is clearing rights!

WHAT PERSONAL QUALITIES DO YOU THINK YOU HAVE THAT HELP IN YOUR JOB?
Enthusiasm for the subject, awareness of the limitations, good people skills and a great deal of patience!

WHAT PRACTICAL ADVICE WOULD YOU GIVE TO SOMEONE WHO WANTED YOUR JOB?
Difficult question as there is no clear career path for this job. I guess I struck lucky. The BBC is the best place to be if you want to make music programmes, so my advice would be to try and get a job in the BBC, as a researcher or production assistant, and make sure that people are aware of your passion for the subject.

7. Record industry

Alongside music publishing, this is the 'business' end of the music industry – finding the musical talent and getting it out to the audiences. There's no doubt that it's an exciting area to work in and very attractive to those who are passionate about music. There are all sorts of areas of work from 'pluggers' and A&R (artists and repertoire) professionals to administrators and lawyers, and competition for all jobs in the sector is fierce.

The 'traditional' model for the recording industry has changed enormously since the beginning of the twenty-first century, and is continuing to evolve at quite a rate. With the advent of MP3s and the ability to download music came a sea change in traditional distribution patterns (which used to be almost entirely CDs sold through record shops). Similarly, where people used to hear about a new band on the radio or TV, or by reading about them in a music magazine, these days they are just as likely to discover a new sound on their friend's playlist on a social networking site. And as high-quality recording equipment has become less expensive (and more accessible), more and more musicians are producing their own recordings and selling them directly to the public (through their own website, for example), or setting up their own independent label.

This doesn't mean that there won't be jobs in this sector in the future, but if you want to work in this area you will need to be forward-thinking and adaptable to make the most of the changes that are inevitably to come. You would do well to do as much research as possible about the industry as it is now, and how it has changed in the recent past (there are plenty of debates and discussions about it online and in magazines and newspapers), to be as open-minded as possible about changes that might come about in the near future.

Any role in the recording industry is going to require you to be passionate about your music, flexible, hardworking and entrepreneurial. There will also be opportunities for people with specialist knowledge – for example in law or marketing. You will also need to be fairly hard-headed: this is an *industry*, after all, and every record label has a responsibility to its shareholders to grow its profits; it may have artistic aims as well, but everyone needs to remember that they are running a business.

A&R

About the job
These are the people working for a record label who are responsible for 'discovering' new talent and persuading them to sign a contract with that company. While some established artists have been around for years, and have a loyal fan base, there is no doubt that the public is always looking for novelty and variety – the next 'big thing'.

A&R executives need to have good artistic and business judgement – they need to know what is selling well for the label and its competitors, and be able to judge whether a new act will fit in with that (or perhaps move the genre on to another stage). They will also need to be able to tell whether an artist has what it takes to make it 'big': not all artists come to a label fully formed and ready to record, and often the A&R department will do a lot of work to develop their sound and/or image before their debut recording is launched. Often, A&R executives will continue to work with artists, helping them to develop their careers even after they have become established, which might include liaison with their A&R counterparts in the music publishing industry to find songs to suit them.

Qualifications
There are no specific qualifications in this field (no degree in 'talent spotting'), but an awful lot of knowledge that needs to be acquired. A general qualification in music (such as one of the excellent courses in popular music that are now available at universities and colleges) can't hurt, but essentially this is a 'learning by doing' occupation. Developing a knowledge base and a track record is going to be important – this means going to as many live performances as possible (A&R executives might attend three or four gigs a night), and keeping on top of the current scene through magazines, blogs, online music sites, social networking and so on. Your knowledge base must also cover the charts – you need to know what is selling, and therefore making money for the record label.

How do I get started?
Start by getting to know as much as you can about the industry (what works financially and artistically for the labels), and by listening to as much

music as you can – both live and recorded. Get out to as many gigs as you can in your local area, and get to know the promoters; learn from them about the artists that are up and coming in your area. Promoting events yourself (for example, setting up a showcase event for fellow students, or an open-mike event at a venue) will be very valuable experience. Develop your social media profile – make sure it's *your* playlist your friends come to when they want to hear new music. This is something you need to keep on top of – little and often is the best way, so that you've always got something new to share. Keep an eye open for opportunities with labels – many now offer internships or similar where you can gain valuable experience and make important contacts. But competition is fierce, so you will need to have the knowledge and background to prove you have what it takes.

MARKETING

About the job
It is the marketing department that is responsible for making sure that the world knows about the recording that is going to be released. While marketing involves publicity (getting information to the press, posters, advertisements on television and radio, etc.) it is about much more than that. Every artist will have a 'target market' – the people the label thinks will buy their recordings. It is up to the marketing department to work out who that market is (their age, social type, income levels, etc.) and how the artist can appeal to them. So that might mean working with stylists to change a group's 'look' or with the producers on what kind of sound the recording will be aiming for.

With artists that are new to a label, the marketing department might work with the A&R executives to develop 'talent' to fit a particular niche. With established artists, they might instead be negotiating with managers or agents, and the artists themselves, to discuss how they might build on what they have already achieved to present something new to their fans without discarding what has made them popular so far. In any case, the marketing department will be working as part of a team, collaborating with others, and willing and able to adapt ideas to fit in with the needs and wishes of others (or to persuade others if their way is likely to be more effective!).

To work in marketing you need to be a good communicator, both for working with the rest of your team and for getting your label's message across. Creativity is another important personality trait for people in marketing – being able to think up new and interesting ways of presenting your information. In addition, you will need to be highly organised, and good IT skills would be helpful as well.

Qualifications
You don't have to have a degree to get started in working in the marketing department of a record label, but it would help (especially if that degree is in something related, such as business or music). In addition, there are various qualifications in marketing that can be obtained from the Chartered Institute of Marketing.

How do I get started?
A good place to start would be to undertake an internship, if you can afford to do so. This wouldn't necessarily have to be within the record industry (although obviously that would be ideal). But marketing skills and knowledge are eminently transferable from one type of company to another. If you have a marketing background, do all you can to improve your music knowledge, so find out about the different record labels: who are their artists? What are the different markets for those artists? What marketing strategies have they used in the past? Equip yourself with any other skills that could be useful (e.g. IT knowledge). Look out for entry-level posts such as administrative assistants within a marketing department.

PLUGGER

About the job
Once an artist's recording is ready, a label will want to get as many people as possible to hear it before it is released, to encourage people to go out and buy it. It is the plugger's job to visit radio and TV stations, and other media outlets, to persuade them to listen to the music and, more importantly, to play it. They might also arrange for artists to perform live on a show, or that the broadcaster could run a competition to win a copy of the CD, a T-shirt, and so on. A plugger needs to have lots of contacts in the media, and be prepared to use them to spread the word about the new recording – so they also need to be charming and persuasive. Pluggers are usually paid per campaign, and often on a commission basis.

Qualifications

This job is going to be just as much about who you know as what you know. You need to be able to visit the right people, and you need them to trust your judgement about what they will want to play on their programmes. As well as knowing about music, you need to be able to 'sell' your artists to the broadcasters, so some kind of background in sales would be an advantage.

SALES AND DISTRIBUTION

About the job

Once the recording has been made, the marketing department has done its job and the plugger has made sure that it has good airplay, hopefully people will want to buy it. So the job of the sales and distribution department is to make sure that vendors have copies of the CDs (music shops, but increasingly other outlets such as supermarkets, both online and in 'real life'), and that the MP3s are circulated to download sites, with the structure in place to collect the income that will create.

Qualifications

There are no specific qualifications that are needed for a sales role, but sales experience is essential. You will need to be efficient, with a very good telephone manner and good interpersonal skills (being able to get on with all sorts of different people).

How do I get started?

You can start to acquire skills in sales techniques in a Saturday job while you're still at school. There are lots of 'tricks of the trade' that can be learned from more experienced sales people (it doesn't necessarily have to be in music – a lot of the skills are the same regardless of what is being sold). Taking jobs in telesales is another good way to gain experience. At the same time, do your research about the record labels – their business model, their markets, their artists.

OTHER JOBS

Music lawyer

The record industry is very big business, and as with any other business there is all sorts of legal paperwork that needs to be completed to make

DEAN MARSH

JOB TITLE
Entertainment lawyer.

JOB DESCRIPTION
Providing legal and business affairs advice; drafting and reviewing agreements; negotiating and structuring of deals; resolving disputes; protection of intellectual property; deal procurement.

WHAT WAS YOUR ROUTE TO THIS JOB?
I trained as a solicitor in a general law firm, then worked as a litigator and gained experience in lots of different areas. I moved into music law after developing a number of contacts in the business who required services, which enabled me to get into a specialist law firm who gave me training. After that, I set up my own firm.

BEST BIT?
Solving problems; helping clients achieve their goals; free music and gigs!

WORST BIT?
The administration.

WHAT PERSONAL QUALITIES DO YOU THINK YOU HAVE THAT HELP IN YOUR JOB?
Good communication skills; creative thinking; an analytical mind; good networking skills ... and stamina!

WHAT PRACTICAL ADVICE WOULD YOU GIVE TO SOMEONE WHO WANTED YOUR JOB?
Get a good degree, preferably in law. Want to be a lawyer first and foremost, not just an entertainment lawyer. Establish contacts. Work in-house in music and other branches of the entertainment industry.

sure that everyone keeps to their obligations, and gets the income they are entitled to. All of this needs someone with very specialised knowledge, which can only be obtained from proper legal training. If you are a keen musician and think this might be the area for you, it will still be necessary to undergo the same training as a lawyer who specialises in any other business or industry, which can be a long and expensive process.

However, for someone who has been trained as a lawyer and who is a keen musician, it can be a great opportunity to use their skills and training in an area they love.

ADMINISTRATION

About the job
All of the jobs above will need administrative staff to support them – the type and number of them will depend on the size of the company. A record company might need accountants and financial administrators, secretaries and PA, technical staff and IT support, personnel, middle management and all the other staff that you would expect to find in any large business. It might be that this is the sort of job you could see yourself doing, and it would be a bonus to you to be doing it within an industry you love; it might be that you aim to work in one of the more specialist areas mentioned above, but working in an administrative capacity could be a good way in to the company.

8. Production

The creation of any kind of recorded or amplified music needs the input of a range of technical staff: record producers, acoustic engineers, sound engineers and more. These sorts of roles might appeal to a musician with creative flair coupled with a good knowledge of physics and/or computing. Music is 'just' sound waves, after all, and someone who understands how they work and how they can be manipulated (and is familiar with the equipment and software to make that happen) can be very useful in the music business – especially if they also understand the artistic side of music-making.

Record producers and sound engineers are key to any music recording; in some types of popular music they might literally put together a track from its constituent parts, helping to create the artist's sound. Some producers extend that remit to taking on the arrangement of the music and being responsible for hiring the session musicians to create the sound they want.

Sound engineers are important 'on the road' as well, as they will be responsible for making sure that the artist's sound is recreated just as they want it at each venue on a tour, so that audiences can be guaranteed a good musical experience every time. Some venues will also employ their own sound engineers, although in smaller establishments this role would probably have to cover other kinds of technical duties as well, such as lighting.

Both studio work and touring can be very exciting in different ways – working with established and up-and-coming musicians, and perhaps being there at the creation of a new musical hit. But they are both very demanding environments. Touring is mentally and physically tiring: the engineer will be one of the first people to arrive at the venue and also one of the last to leave as all the equipment must be taken down and safely packed away ready to be taken to the next show. Studio work has its own demands, as it is both a technical and creative process, and a lot relies on the artist being able to deliver what's needed at the time. Some studio sessions might start in the late morning and then go on into the early (or even late!) hours of the following morning, and the technical staff need to be able to work as a team and give the artist what they need. As with any collaborative role, personality is going to be important – if you get on well with everyone and work hard to benefit the recording rather than just yourself you will be valued. As Lyndon Jones, freelance media producer, puts it: 'Being able to establish good, positive working relationships quickly is important and valuable … good manners are surprisingly useful. But you do need to know what you're doing, and do it well; if you're blagging it, people generally don't take long to cotton on.'

PRODUCER

About the job
The producer is the creative leader behind a recording. The amount of input he or she has will depend on the type of music and the performing artists, but it might vary from working collaboratively with someone with an artistic vision (for example, with the conductor of an orchestra) to being in sole charge of every aspect of the music produced, including choosing the songs and musicians (as in some pop music recordings).

The producer will usually have excellent technical knowledge – he or she will often have staff to put things into practice, but will have to know just what sounds and effects are available to the artist, and how to make those happen. It is often the producer, though, who can advise the artist on how a song can be shaped, arranged, or otherwise improved. So their role is creative as well as technical.

Great producers are as revered in the music business as great performers are. It's perhaps not a job to be thinking of aiming for straight away, but a long-term goal for the technically and creatively talented.

Qualifications
Rather than qualifications as such, there are various skills to be acquired for this role, which might be taught in a formal environment or could also be self-taught or learnt 'on the job' either as an engineer or as a recording artist.

To begin with, technical knowledge must be acquired. As freelance sound technician and producer James Shears tells us, 'the physics of what we do has never and will never change!' So some education in physics would be useful, as would education on the various kinds of software that are

MARTIN WRIGHT

JOB TITLE
I am a producer/musician/writer, and also teach higher education.

JOB DESCRIPTION
My job is varied and changes from day to day, which is something I always wanted from the very beginning of my career in music. I find myself having to put on many different hats to suit the needs of clients that require any of the skills I have acquired over the many years working in music. These will range from playing drums on a record, performing live with various musicians where I'll be asked to sing lead or backing vocals as well, writing music in bands or for synchronisation and for my own projects, as well as producing young and old artists, mixing and mastering songs and albums, to teaching and even teaching people how to teach.

WHAT WAS YOUR ROUTE TO THIS JOB?
I started playing drums at the age of 11 and quickly found myself playing in blues bands with players old enough to be my father. That continued to be my weekend job while I was at secondary school. I went to sixth-form college to study photography and drama, but had already made my mind up at that stage about wanting to do something in music. My first big recording in a studio when I was 17 with a producer blew my mind. I was fascinated with how he crafted our songs into polished recordings. From that moment I was obsessed with all things studio. I gained a place on one of the first modern music courses in London at the age of 20 and studied for two years, learning many different sides of the industry. This encouraged me to sing, write, produce and play, so I stayed in London for 15 years working in bands, making records for a real mix of artists, touring both here and abroad with some amazing musicians.

BEST BIT?
The variety is great. It keeps me on my toes and I never get bored of my work. There is something magical about hearing a song for the first time and the possibilities for how that song could end up. That whole process from beginning to end is probably the most inspiring part of my work: being part of creating something that never existed before.

WORST BIT?
Nothing!

available to music producers (and as with any software these will change all the time, so there is a need to keep up to date). Then there are all the different types of recording and amplification equipment that will be used – a producer needs a knowledge of all of these and what all the various knobs on the mixing desk mean and do. There are now some courses that give a grounding in all of this technical knowledge.

Musical ability will also be vital. This doesn't necessarily mean that the producer will need to be able to play an instrument (although that wouldn't hurt), but that he or she needs to understand how harmony works; how a melody could be extended or improved; why the structure of a song isn't quite working and what can be done to improve it.

How do I get started?
To begin working your way up in this area of the business, be thinking about improving your technical and musical skills right from when you're in school. Work hard at your compositions and try to take any opportunity to familiarise yourself with a new type of recording software. Try to find ways of finding out about the technical equipment and processes – offer to help friends who are in bands with their equipment, or volunteer at your local small venue (like a pub or a club), perhaps. Be a willing and enthusiastic extra pair of hands, and try to use the time to learn as much as you can from the 'old hands'.

Getting into a studio will be the next step. Again, take any opportunity that presents itself – whether it's tidying up at the end of a session or making the tea. Be enthusiastic and hard-working, putting yourself out for the staff. Watch, listen and learn, and you'll be on your way to a role as an assistant engineer or technician.

STUDIO SOUND ENGINEER

About the job
The sound engineer is responsible for making sure the studio is set up and operating the equipment during the recording session; he or she might also be asked to run the recording session (who does what when; which takes could be used) and/or mix down the track after the session. There may be one or more assistants to whom he or she can delegate tasks.

Qualifications

The sound engineer will need to be the technical expert, which will involve acquiring all the skills mentioned above for the producer's role. So it's important to have a good knowledge of all the hardware and software used in the recording process, and also to keep abreast of new developments and products coming in, as the technology is improving all the time. There are a number of sound production colleges at higher education level, which could give you an excellent grounding, but you will also have to take responsibility for educating yourself by getting as much experience and practice as possible, reading trade magazines, and so on. Traditionally (and this continues today) sound engineers start off as assistant engineers (or tape operators). Effectively this is an apprenticeship and either is an alternative to or complements formal training.

A good musical ear is also a vital attribute. You need to be able to hear that the drummer was slightly late on one of the tracks, or that the guitar has slipped out of tune, for example, and so ask for a new take. If you are mixing, you will need to be able to hear all the elements of the track separately and together, and have a good aesthetic sense of how things are balanced. So as well as a good musical training (academic and/or practical), you will need to do lots of close critical listening to recorded music to get an idea of how other people approach the task, and what you might want to do the same or differently.

How do I get started?

A good grounding in music and physics would be useful to begin with, possibly followed by a higher education course in sound production. There are other useful avenues as well: for example, sound technician and producer James Shears spent some time working in the technical sales department for a manufacturer of audio equipment to the music industry, and then moved into the design and development of mixing consoles for that company – that high level of technical expertise will be very attractive to studio managers looking for a new engineer.

The same advice follows as for the production role: use any opportunity to gain experience. Perhaps you have friends in bands who want some help putting together a demo recording, or you can help with the sound for your local theatre, for example.

LIVE SOUND ENGINEER

About the job

The live sound engineer is the person responsible for every aspect of the sound production for an artist's live performance – working out what equipment is necessary, setting it up before the gig (arranging placements of mics, speakers, etc.), getting the mix right during sound check (and sometimes mixing during the live performance, adding in special effects, etc.), then making sure the equipment is taken down and safely packed away at the end of the performance. For small events, this might all be one person's job, but for larger events there might be a team of assistants and roadies to help – but the engineer will be responsible for making sure things get done.

The aim of the job is to help the artist produce the sound they want consistently, night after night, in venues that might vary enormously in terms of size and acoustic properties (how the sound behaves in the space). Some artists will have a very clear idea of what they want, and will expect to work in collaboration with the engineer to achieve that; others might be happy to leave everything in the engineer's hands (as long as they trust him or her to do a good job for them).

In addition to the front-of-house engineer, larger bands will have a separate monitor engineer. His or her job is to make sure that the band can hear the instruments and vocals on stage. Each band member will have a separate loudspeaker (or in-ear speakers) and can have their own personal mix of the instruments and vocals to help them give a good performance.

The sound engineer needs to be hard-working, calm in a crisis and utterly reliable, because if something goes a little bit wrong (for example a guitarist getting a bit too close to a speaker and setting off a squeal of feedback) you will need to deal with it quickly and with the minimum amount of fuss. You also have to be happy to work long, antisocial hours (more often than not at the weekend) and be away from home for extended periods of time.

Qualifications, and how do I get started?

All the advice as given above for production and sound engineering would apply here also, but in addition try to get as much experience as possible with live sound in venues of different shapes and sizes. Try to learn about what attributes affect the sound, such as the height and length of the

DARIUS KEDROS

JOB TITLE
Live sound engineer

JOB DESCRIPTION
I mix the band's sound for the audience at concerts.

WHAT WAS YOUR ROUTE TO THIS JOB?
After college I got a lucky break with a job in a rehearsal room in London, which taught me the basics of sound engineering live music. I used to go the extra mile and make rehearsal recordings for bands that I liked, which got me noticed, and so I started getting hired to do gigs, and then tours and festivals.

BEST BIT?
Being creatively involved with the show, flying in dubby effects like reverbs and echoes is very rewarding. But also just getting a great sound is very satisfying in itself. I also like seeing parts of the world (albeit briefly quite often) that I would not have otherwise visited (Japan, USA, etc.).

WORST BIT?
Being away from my wife and kids for more than a week or two can be really hard on them and me. Touring is also hard work, and can lack private 'me time'.

WHAT PERSONAL QUALITIES DO YOU THINK YOU HAVE THAT HELP IN YOUR JOB?
I am quite a confident person, and I think that helps bands, managers and tour managers to trust in me and my abilities. I am also pretty easy-going, and up for a giggle when the time is right, but I am conscientious about my work, and take it seriously.

WHAT PRACTICAL ADVICE WOULD YOU GIVE TO SOMEONE WHO WANTED YOUR JOB?
If you want to mix live music you must first be good at it, and that takes practice, but also you need to know bands, band managers and tour managers because they are the people that hire you. So, do as much networking as you can manage, and always have business cards with you.

Start working in small venues like pubs, clubs and theatres that put on live music, and try to get work with PA companies too.

room, number of people in it, material used to make the floor or walls (wood reacts very differently from stone, for example) and so on. You can learn some of this out of books, but you will also need to experience it for yourself and hear the differences in sound in real life, as well as learning the different things you can do to counteract the challenges the space presents to you.

OTHER JOBS

Assistants roles
Producers, engineers and technicians need assistants. For production, this might be more administrative (booking musicians, scheduling studio time, etc.), and a lot of it will be doing the 'leg-work' of the job: checking microphones, taping cables down, and so on. Larger studios might also employ people for specific parts of the production/engineering job, such as studio setup.

Post-production
After tracks have been recorded, they need to be mixed and finalised, and this part of the process (post-production) can make a considerable difference to the sound. Some engineers specialise in this aspect of production away from the recording studio and might also then be working on post-production of other types of recordings (such as spoken sound for TV and film).

Studio staff
Smaller studios might be just a producer with his or her recording space, but larger operations might employ a number of people, so there could be openings for other administrative types of work, such as managing the studio's schedule, dealing with the accounts, and so on.

Musical equipment hire
Producers and studios don't necessarily own all the equipment they need – they might want to hire extra equipment from time to time. Bands on tour will also probably want to hire equipment to take with them. Working for one of the many companies that hires equipment out could be an excellent way to get a really thorough knowledge of the options available and how they work.

9. Retailing

Until not very long ago, music retailing – in this instance, 'record shops' – was one of the most important areas of work for anyone serious about working in the music industry. It was a common career path for someone to start as a sales assistant for a big chain of shops, work their way up to being a buyer and then use those contacts to move into the record business, perhaps in A&R. Since the beginning of the twenty-first century, however, the whole profile of the retailing sector has changed rapidly. First, people started buying their CDs in other places, such as supermarkets; then came the boom in online retailers, who were able to cut prices by having fewer overheads (costs); then sales in CDs themselves started to drop as more and more people started buying their music as MP3 downloads.

This doesn't mean that record shops have died out entirely, but the shops are less dominating and more 'niche' than they used to be. There are also opportunities, of course, in working for the online retailers. But it isn't just music recordings retailing covers – there are also specialist music shops selling instruments and sheet music of various kinds. At the very specialist end, there are the people who make the instruments to be sold.

Depending on the size of the retailer, the work might be split up into different roles, or one or two people might be expected to do everything. To begin with, there has to be a **buyer** – someone who decides what the shop will be selling, and hopefully buys just the right amount of stock so that you have what people want to buy, and don't have loads left over taking up space. Next, someone has to arrange the stock so that it looks attractive and so customers can find what they need, perhaps putting up displays for special promotions; this is called **merchandising**. Then, of course, someone has to serve the customers; a **sales assistant** also needs to be knowledgeable about the products, so that he or she can give advice to the customers. Often there will need to be a **manager** as well (who might also be the shop owner), who will organise everything, and keep on top of the financial side of things to make sure that the money coming in is more than the money going out (on rent, wages, stock, etc.). The larger retail chains, and online stores, will also have jobs for people in administration, accounting, IT, and so on.

QUALIFICATIONS

There aren't necessarily any specific qualifications needed to work in retailing – indeed, many people start working part time as a sales assistant when they're still at school. But if you want to work in a specialist music shop you will need to have the knowledge to be able to advise customers, and that is probably something you will have to acquire in your own time. There are courses (and degrees) in retail, which is a possible road in for someone keen to pursue a retailing career, but these will not be specific to music. Some larger organisations, such as HMV, have graduate training schemes.

Most people working in retail will also need the skills to deal with customers (some of whom can be difficult and/or rude at times), so the ability to keep smiling no matter what, and to be calm and patient, is vital. It's not the most lucrative of occupations, and standing at a till all day being pleasant to people can be remarkably tiring, but often you get to spend a lot of your day talking about your passion (music), and helping other people to enjoy it, and what could be better than that?

HOW DO I GET STARTED?

As mentioned above, the best place to start is probably a weekend job in a shop while you're still at school. At this point in time, it doesn't matter so much if this isn't in a music-related shop – it's the experience of the retail environment that's important. At the same time, you'll need to be acquiring the specialist knowledge – which could be dance music for that specialist vinyl shop or brass playing for the specialist instrument shop.

For the larger organisations there will be advertisements for openings and training schemes; for the smaller concerns, it might just be a question of being a regular customer, getting to know the staff and management, sharing your passion, and letting them know you're looking for work should the opportunity arise.

Another possible way in to retailing is to start up your own shop, either real or virtual. This is not something to be entered into lightly as it will require a certain amount of capital (financial investment) that could all be lost if the venture fails. If this is something you are thinking about, and you have the money to invest, seek out good advice (there are lots of useful websites), and do your research – is there really enough demand for what you want to sell to create enough income? Be realistic about what your overheads will be and make sure you create a comprehensive business plan before you start – your bank's business manager might be able to give help and advice here.

TYPES OF MUSIC SHOPS

Record shops

Most of these shops now sell CDs rather than records (vinyl), but the name seems to have stuck. Many of the general record shops (such as the large chains) have diversified to increase their potential income, so also sell DVDs, books, posters, T-shirts, and so on. Some shops will specialise in a particular kind of music, such as classical music or vinyl for DJs. There's also a specialist market for vintage vinyl, which has become a collector's item.

Customers coming to specialist record shops will expect the staff to have an in-depth knowledge, and many of them will hope to have interesting conversations about their favourite artists, so this could be just the job for you if your family and friends have got fed up with hearing you talk about the relative merits of Jack White or Andrew White on lead guitar, or give a detailed analysis of Tinie Tempah's lyrics.

Sheet music

Most musicians will want to buy sheet music at some point or another, whether the score of an oratorio, a songbook with guitar tab for an album that has just been released, or a book of beginner pieces for the piano. Shops that sell sheet music also sell related items such as manuscript paper, theory books, and so on. Once again, the customers to this sort of shop will expect a certain amount of knowledge, but it needs to be somewhat broader – you will need to know where on the shelves Mozart's 'Rondo alla Turca' can be found, and where to look for the guitar tab for 'Killing Me Softly', so a good general knowledge of lots of different genres is required.

Instruments

People who want to buy instruments will generally want to try them out first. No two instruments are ever identical, even if they were made by the same people in the same factory, and players will try quite a few before they find the one that fits them (a bit like the young wizards trying to find the right wand in *Harry Potter*). There are general instrument shops, selling a large range, who tend to cater for the beginner and hobbyist end of the market (slightly less expensive), and specialist shops who might only sell string instruments, or pianos, or electric guitars – this is where you will find a lot of the more expensive instruments. These shops will also sell the various extra bits and pieces the instruments need – cases, reeds, strings, stands, cleaning equipment, and so on. A lot of these shops also deal with repairs, and buy and sell second-hand instruments.

General music shops

Some shops do all of the above: selling instruments, accessories, sheet music, recordings – basically anything to do with music! To work in a shop like this you would need to have a very good all-round knowledge, perhaps also with a specialism in one particular area.

Instrument-making

At some point, the instruments to be sold need to be created. A lot now come from factories in places like China, but there is still a small market for specialist handmade instruments. Making instruments is a craft that can take many years of learning and practice to master, and really needs to be acquired over a long period of time in an apprenticeship. As well as being a good musician with an excellent ear, you need to be practical and good with your hands, and something of a perfectionist. Being a luthier or an organ-maker is never going to make you rich, but it is a craft that can make your life very meaningful, doing something that you love. If you think this could be what you want to do, find out who makes the instrument you play, and approach them to see if they offer apprenticeships, or where they would suggest you look for training.

WILLIAM RING

JOB TITLE
I work for Howarth of London Ltd as IT manager in the manufacturing department and am also marketing manager. Howarth of London is known for the manufacture and retail of woodwind instruments and their accessories.

JOB DESCRIPTION
I fulfil a number of roles, as a result of having a small management team within a company of 50+ employees, of whom the majority are actually manufacturing instruments. They include IT and marketing, which means creating artwork for publicity, but also having a hand in product development, both of new ranges (e.g. the junior range of instruments specifically for the younger beginner), and developments of existing technologies and instruments (e.g. a twenty-first-century oboe, featured in *Classical Music* magazine).

WHAT WAS YOUR ROUTE TO THIS JOB?
My parents were professional musicians specialising in period instruments, where the aspect of making 'authentic' instruments is much closer to the process of playing them than in more 'classical' environments; as such, making instruments was always an interest from my teenage years onwards. I also enjoyed model-making as I grew up. Between school and university I had the opportunity to work making woodwind instruments in Germany, then studied music at university. After university I spent a year making instruments in France, then – by dint of a chance phone call – was able to interview for a job at Howarth in 1981.

BEST BIT?
All of it! The range of things I cover is part of the stimulus, but there are also good opportunities to be creative, which is not necessarily the case for many of the actual production staff, who need to be able to do a quite complex job efficiently and very skilfully.

WORST BIT?
Paper admin! It's less bad if it's done on screen, but it's so easy to accumulate piles of paper around my desk!

WHAT PERSONAL QUALITIES DO YOU THINK YOU HAVE THAT HELP IN YOUR JOB?
Flexibility, ability to keep several threads going at once, ability to see connections in all sorts of places. I think in graphical terms (as opposed to conceptually), and I enjoy physical creativity (making things!).

I have also been lucky enough to gain a lot of transferable skills over time, including an interest in IT and being tri-lingual, which I still use for work.

WHAT PRACTICAL ADVICE WOULD YOU GIVE TO SOMEONE WHO WANTED YOUR JOB?
Push doors and expect to start at the bottom. (Having spent time working through all the processes/departments in the manufacturing workshops I have a better understanding of the many related issues involved in development.) It can be useful to have been to one of the instrument-making/repairing courses, but we usually need to give significant (re)training to bring staff up to the commercial speed and quality we require.

In the manufacturing workshops a good craft skill with dexterity and an eye for detail are more important than 'creativity'. In the sales department in London, the requirement is an ability to play one – and be knowledgeable about at least one – of the woodwind family that we sell, and then to have good retail skills, a personable manner, and so on.

PIANO TUNER

This occupation isn't technically retailing, but is included here as a number of piano tuners align themselves with piano salesrooms. Upright and grand pianos (but not electronic ones) need to be tuned on a regular basis to keep them in good condition. As well as checking and maintaining the pitch of the instrument, a piano tuner will sort out other aspects of its mechanism (such as the pedals).

A piano tuner needs to have an extremely good ear, as well as practical skills and the people skills to be comfortable going into people's homes. Most are self-employed or freelance. The occupation has traditionally been one that could be carried out by visually impaired people, and the Royal National College for the Blind still offers training courses, as does the London College of Furniture.

10. Pathways and applications

MUSIC QUALIFICATIONS

There is now a good range of qualifications in music, encompassing academic and practical skills in all sorts of different genres. The kind of qualifications you will want to obtain will depend on your chosen career, your own particular strengths and weaknesses, and your personality.

Academic qualifications
If you are suited to the more academic side of music, you could begin with a GCSE and A level in music, before moving on to university for a bachelor's degree (such as a BA) in music. This would be a good starting point for careers such as arts administration or teaching, which require a good general knowledge of classical music. If you find that academic learning suits you, or you want to follow a specialism such as classical composition, you might choose to move on to a postgraduate degree (an MA, then perhaps a PhD).

These courses might contain a small performance element, but they are mostly concentrated on other musical skills (music history, analysis, composition, etc.). A degree in music is just as valuable in the workplace as a degree in any other arts or humanities subject, and in that respect it might be a good choice for someone who isn't quite sure what path they will follow later.

Classical performance
If you are a budding classical instrumentalist or singer, the pathway is fairly clear. Most will have a Grade 8 distinction from an examining board (such as the ABRSM or Trinity College London) as a starting point, and will study at a music college or conservatoire (such as one of the Royal Schools of Music). Most conservatoires now award a BMus degree, although there are diplomas that can also be obtained, such as the Licentiate of the Royal

Academy of Music (LRAM). The examining boards now offer practical music diplomas as well, such as the Licentiate of the Royal Schools of Music (LRSM) or the Licentiate of Trinity College London (LTCL). The conservatoires also have postgraduate courses, offering further study for people who have already completed a first performance degree, or who have a different degree but with a similar level of performance ability (e.g. LRSM level).

This is a fairly narrow route to follow. The courses will teach other skills along the way, such as education and outreach work, and will give a good general grounding in music, but essentially they are focused on producing excellent performers who will be able to find work as ensemble players or soloists.

Popular music performance

If you want to work as a musician or singer in a popular music genre, there is nothing to stop you doing just that – you don't necessarily need a qualification. However, there are now a number of great courses that can improve your performance skills while giving you a helpful understanding of how the industry operates, how best to market yourself, and so on.

Most further education colleges will offer courses in music, usually working towards a recognised vocational qualification (e.g. City & Guilds award, or BTEC), which can lead to a National Vocational Qualification (NVQ).

There are then colleges dedicated to working in popular music, such as the Brighton Institute of Modern Music (BIMM). These offer a range of options from part-time courses working towards an NVQ, up to undergraduate and even postgraduate degrees. The great thing about a dedicated popular music college is that as a performer you will be studying alongside people who are training in the other aspects of the industry (such as production and business); it will be a good starting point for making the contacts you will need further on in your career. Also, the teaching staff at these colleges are often industry insiders who have a great deal of experience behind them to share with the students.

Production and music technology

If music technology is what interests you – perhaps with the aim of working as an engineer or producer – there is a whole range of courses. There are music technology options for A level, and then it is possible to take college courses towards NVQs, or undergraduate then postgraduate degrees. The direction you travel along this route will depend upon your preferred learning style. If you learn better by doing, the vocational paths will probably suit you better; some college courses are run part-time so that you can study while you are working. If you get on well with maths and physics, and enjoy learning the science behind the equipment, a degree course might be a better option for you.

Music management and business
While some people may choose to take a degree in business studies (which should teach skills that are applicable in any area of business), increasingly, dedicated music business management courses are becoming popular. The advantage of these, of course, is that the skills and knowledge most appropriate to the music business can be taught throughout. There are the same kinds of vocational and degree options that are available for the music technology courses.

The university of life
You will have read in a number of the case studies in this book that people had a qualification in something completely different from music, or no qualifications at all. Certainly, in the past, it was very common for young people to go directly into work after leaving school, at 16 or 18, and to learn on the job. As jobs have become harder to come by (especially in the popular field of the music industry), this has become more and more difficult to do. It *is* still possible with an enormous amount of hard work and determination, and no small amount of luck, to find your way into the business in some areas without any kind of qualification, but it's a risky path to follow: for every self-taught music engineer there will be count-less, perhaps hundreds, of people who really wanted to do it and tried their best but ended up not being able to find their way in, and doing something else. The 'university of life' route is probably best followed only if you really cannot stand studying for any longer and/or you have managed to secure yourself an entry-level position in your chosen area of work from which to build.

Other things employers will want to see
This has been mentioned throughout the book, but it is worth stressing it again here. Qualifications on their own will probably not be enough to get you the job you want. Even if you manage to get, say, a first-class degree in music production, when a job at a top studio comes up there will be plenty of other people who also have a first-class degree. You need to be able to prove to a potential employer that you are passionate about,

and dedicated to, music and whatever career it is that you want to follow. This isn't something a college course will be able to give you (although a number of the colleges do great work in helping their students to find work experience and similar) – you will have to be self-motivated and do everything you can to get as much experience behind you.

To begin with, do your research. This might be finding out everything you can about artists in a particular field, or keeping up to date with the latest developments in recording equipment, or whatever is relevant to the job you want. The internet is a wonderful resource; choose your search terms carefully to make sure you get the pages you want straight away. For example, a search on Google for 'labels' gives nearly 600 million hits, none of which on the first two pages are of any use; a search for 'list record labels UK' provides almost 8 million hits, but there are six different directories of record labels (including their contact details) in the UK on the first page. You will also find lists of useful websites, grouped like the chapters in this book, on the Rhinegold Education website, to get you started.

The other important thing to do is to get as much experience as you can. Be prepared to use your spare time to help other people with equipment at their gigs, or volunteer for hospital radio, or help with stewarding at local concerts, or any of the other suggestions that have been made through-out this book. Later down the line, pursue opportunities for internships in companies in your chosen field – a spell as an intern is rapidly becoming a 'must-have' for CVs in all areas of the creative industries. This experience will not only show potential employers that you are keen, it will also show you what the job really entails, and enable you to decide if it is what you really want to do with your life.

APPLYING FOR JOBS

Where to look for work
You will need to look in a number of different places for job opportunities. Advertisements might be placed on job search sites, newspaper/magazine jobs pages, or on the employer's own website, or the company's own website. Often, jobs can be found where they haven't even been advertised (see 'speculative approaches', on page 99).

To begin with, visit the websites of organisations you would like to work for, to see if they have job opportunities posted on their own websites. If they do, bookmark these pages and go back to visit them regularly. Do your research to find other organisations in the same field and bookmark any job vacancy pages they have as well.

Next, find the websites that list vacancies in your field from lots of different organisations (the Rhinegold Education website has some suggestions to start you off, but use a search engine and careful search terms to find others), and bookmark these as well. It would be worth visiting these very day, as the jobs listed here will change more quickly than those from a single organisation. Read around on the site to find out what the organisation does – some will just be advertisement listings, but others will be recruitment agencies, who might give you the option of sending them your CV so that they have your details on file for potential employers. If you live close enough to the recruitment agency's office, it would be worth you taking in your CV personally, as you will be more memorable to the agency's staff if they can put a face to the name. In addition, they will be well placed to give you advice on what you can be doing to make yourself more attractive to employers.

Jobs are also listed in newspapers and specialist magazines. Some of these will be more general (for example the *Guardian* newspaper lists 'media' and 'arts' jobs), whereas others will be more specialised in a particular area (e.g. *Music Week* lists music management jobs). Once again, there are some suggestions on the Rhinegold Education website to start you off, but hopefully you will be reading the magazines in your area anyway, to keep you up to date with new developments.

Networking
Networking will be an important part of many people's job search. This means getting out to places where you can meet people already in the industry, and it is a chance to get your name and face familiar with people who might be in a position to give you a job one day. For musicians, this might mean gigs, or perhaps open meetings about the future of the industry. Seminars and day courses are also useful networking opportunities, and sometimes organisations such as magazines hold open events where there is a chance to meet the staff. Any voluntary work or internships you might have done would also be excellent networking. To have a chance of making a good impression, be friendly and professional. Make sure you introduce yourself clearly ('Hello, my name is Sarah Jones

and I'm an aspiring sound engineer'), and be prepared to talk about yourself if asked, but it is more important to ask questions. This is your opportunity to find out from the horse's mouth about the organisation or the industry, and most people will be very happy to talk about it. You want to be remembered as the person who seemed keen and interested, not the egotist who just wanted to talk about themselves all the time. This is also the way that you're going to find out very useful inside information about the industry.

Online social networking might also be an important tool in the job search; for some, such as aspiring singer-songwriters, it will be vital. You will need to decide for yourself which sites are going to be more relevant to you (e.g. MySpace for aspiring performers, or LinkedIn for fledgling magazine editors), but the principles will be the same. Writing a blog would come into this category as well. Here are some tips to help make the most of your social networking:

- You can link up all your sites so that when you post a new track on MySpace, say, you share that information with your Facebook profile and your Twitter feed to get maximum coverage. Little and often is important – rather than a huge post every now and then, try to find one little thing to say every day.
- Don't make it all about you! People will soon get fed up with your posts if they're always trumpeting your own achievements. Be generous – retweet someone else's funny link; share a new track you've just heard that you really like on MySpace; link to someone's interesting blog. If you do a good deed for someone else they are more likely to do the same for you, and when you *do* post something about yourself people will be more inclined to read it and take note. Keep it professional. If you are a singer, for example, create a fan page for your business and keep it strictly separate from your personal page. By all means encourage all your personal friends to like it, but don't, whatever you do, post pictures of yourself dancing on the table at your friend's birthday party.

If you have the technical ability, you might also want to consider setting up a personal website, where you can also have your background/education and work experience, photos, sample MP3s for download, contact form and so on. If you decide to go down this route, make sure it looks professional and works well on all the different browsers, and make sure the URL is as simple and memorable as possible, as well as being professional (in other words, if you are hoping to become a music manager, the

URL http://genericwebsite/personal/dir_4263/sparklybunnies probably wouldn't be a good idea; it would be much better to try to get hold of the domain name www.yournamemanagement.co.uk or similar). If you're not confident in your own technical ability to do a good job, it would be a worthwhile investment to get a website designer to set something up for you; many will set up a site for a fixed fee, and then show you how to update the content, which you should do on a regular basis.

Speculative approaches

A great many jobs are not advertised at all. Putting out an advertisement, sorting through all the responses to make a shortlist, then interviewing prospective candidates all costs a company time and money that they often prefer to save by offering the job to someone they know anyway. Note that this doesn't apply to some jobs, which by law have to be advertised (e.g. jobs in the public sector).

The first step will be to do your research – find out which organisations are most likely to have the sort of job you want, and then find out as much as you can about them, including the name of the person who would be your boss if you got a job there. Use any contacts you have made through networking as well here – ask their advice, or put them on the list themselves. Look particularly for organisations that will be more likely to be hiring new staff – perhaps they have just taken on a big new client, or are moving to new premises.

The next thing to do is to adapt your CV to suit that particular organisation. Some things on your CV will stay the same, of course, such as personal contact details and educational history, but think carefully about which of your skills and experiences would be most useful to the organisation and make sure you highlight those.

Now write a letter to your contact – address them by name, and sign the letter 'Yours sincerely'. Double-check that you have copied down the name of the contact correctly; then check it again, very carefully. You can send the letter by post or in an email with your CV as an attachment. (Note: unsolicited emails with attachments are often diverted into 'junk' folders by spam filters – when you make your follow-up telephone call the first thing you should do is check that it has arrived. If you have your CV online, you could include a link to it in your email rather than attaching it to the message.) Show that you have researched the company (e.g. 'I was very interested to read in *Music Week* on 9 October that MusicCorp will be moving to larger premises'), and explain briefly why you would like to work for them in particular. Give a brief overview of your skills and experiences, referring to your CV for further information, and explain that you would like to come in to meet them to discuss potential opportunities. Promise to telephone on a particular date (say, a week later) to follow up the letter, and then remember to make that telephone call! If, when you call, the contact says that they will not be taking on new staff at that time, you could still ask for a meeting – it is a good opportunity to ask questions about the company, and the industry as a whole, and also to gain feedback on your CV – is there anything they think you should change? Is there anything else you could be doing to enhance your skills and experience?

If your application is not successful, ask if you might contact them again in, say, three months' time. Also, include the person you met on any professional social network (e.g. invite them to link with you on LinkedIn).

Tips on applications
Your CV is the document that must sell you to a potential employer. There are a few golden rules:

- Keep it concise – no more than two sides of A4.
- Use a neat, clear layout, with no fancy gimmicks or flowery fonts (and definitely don't use Comic Sans). Don't use more than two different fonts (e.g. one for headings and a different one for the main text).
- Open the CV with a short personal statement about who you are and what you are looking for (for example, 'Hard-working music graduate with a passion for PR looking for an entry-level position in the music industry').
- Proofread it carefully, and ask someone knowledgeable to proofread it for you as well – a spelling mistake could be the cause of it ending up in the recycling bin.
- Create separate sections for: personal contact details, education and qualifications, work experience/voluntary work, other information (e.g. transferable skills, other qualifications such as driving licence, personal interests/hobbies), referees (make sure you check first that people are happy to act as referees for you).
- Make sure that you customise the CV for every job you apply for or speculative approach you make, so that the skills and experiences that are most relevant are more prominent.

- If you are sending your CV out in an electronic format (as an email attachment), don't send it as a word processor file (such as a .doc file or .rtf file); save it as a pdf or similar – that way, when it is opened at the other end you can be sure that it will look exactly as it did when you sent it.

Keep the CV factual, but try to make clear exactly what your experience has taught you that will be useful to your potential employer (e.g. 'member of amateur theatre group: this gave me experience of operating sound playback equipment in a live context, as well as teaching me valuable lessons about working in a small team').

When you are applying for a particular job, always include a covering letter and make sure that the job title and any reference number are clearly noted at the top (usually on a line of its own, after the 'Dear Ms Smith' – you might want to centre it and put it in bold for prominence). State briefly why you are applying to the post, refer to your CV, and draw together some of the threads of your experience (e.g. 'As you will see from the enclosed CV, as well as a strong academic education, I have taken every opportunity to experience music-therapy work in a practical context, which has cemented my desire to work in the sector'). Don't try to include everything in your CV in the letter as well, but use this chance to draw their attention to the most important parts. Finish with a statement explaining why you think you could be of benefit to the organisation – be confident, but don't brag – and say that you will look forward to hearing from them.

Index of job titles